ANGER AND DETACHMENT

A Study of Arden, Osborne and Pinter

Michael Anderson

Pitman Publishing

First published 1976

PITMAN PUBLISHING LTD
Pitman House, 39 Parker Street, London WC2B 5PB, UK

PITMAN MEDICAL PUBLISHING CO LTD
42 Camden Road, Tunbridge Wells, Kent TN1 2QD, UK

FOCAL PRESS LTD
31 Fitzroy Square, London W1P 6BH, UK

PITMAN PUBLISHING CORPORATION
6 East 43 Street, New York, NY 10017, USA

FEARON PUBLISHERS INC
6 Davis Drive, Belmont, California 94002, USA

PITMAN PUBLISHING PTY LTD
Pitman House, 158 Bouverie Street, Carlton, Victoria 3053, Australia

PITMAN PUBLISHING
COPP CLARK PUBLISHING
517 Wellington Street West, Toronto M5V 1G1, Canada

SIR ISAAC PITMAN AND SONS LTD
Banda Street, PO Box 46038, Nairobi, Kenya

PITMAN PUBLISHING CO SA (PTY) LTD
Craighall Mews, Jan Smuts Avenue, Craighall Park, Johannesburg 2001, South Africa

Cased edition ISBN: 0 273 00353 4
Paperback edition ISBN: 0 273 00257 0

Text set in 10/11 pt. Photon Imprint, printed by photolithography, and bound in Great Britain at The Pitman Press, Bath

G3544/3507: 15

ANGER AND DETACHMENT
A Study of Arden, Osborne and Pinter

Contents

Acknowledgements

I am very grateful to all those who have given me permission to quote from published works, in particular the following:

John Arden, from *The Waters of Babylon* and *Live Like Pigs*, published in *Three Plays* by Penguin Books Ltd, and from *Telling a True Tale*, published in *The Encore Reader* by Eyre Methuen Ltd and shorter extracts from other works.
John Arden and Margaretta D'Arcy, from *The Island of the Mighty*, published by Eyre Methuen and shorter extracts from other works.

John Osborne, from *Look Back in Anger, Epitaph for George Dillon* (with Anthony Creighton), *The Entertainer, The World of Paul Slickey, The Blood of the Bambergs, Inadmissible Evidence, Time Present, The Hotel in Amsterdam, The Right Prospectus, West of Suez* and *A Place Calling Itself Rome*, all published by Faber and Faber Ltd and shorter extracts from other works.

Harold Pinter, from *The Tea Party, The Room, The Birthday Party, The Homecoming* and *Landscape*, all published by Eyre Methuen and shorter extracts from other works.

M.A.

1 Critical approaches

John Osborne, John Arden and Harold Pinter all began their careers as playwrights in the second half of the 1950s, during a period that is generally regarded as a turning-point for English drama. It is too early for a final assessment of any of them—all three, after all, are still in their forties—but the time is ripe, it seems to me, for a fresh look at what they have written so far. In the mind of the general public they are probably best known for their early plays: *Look Back in Anger* and *The Entertainer*; *Serjeant Musgrave's Dance*; *The Birthday Party* and *The Caretaker*; but since then each of them has continued to develop, ringing the changes on their earlier themes and subjects, refining some features, rejecting others, and directing their attention to new areas of experience as their own artistic personalities mature; and many of the judgements which were formed on the basis of their earlier work are now due for revision. *West of Suez* and *A Sense of Detachment* are recognizably plays by the author of *Look Back in Anger*, but equally clearly they reflect a different temperament, grappling with concerns which are not quite the same as those that affected the 'angry young man' of fifteen years before. Similarly *The Ballygombeen Bequest* has its affinities with *Serjeant Musgrave's Dance*, but the later play contains an element of political commitment which Arden had steadfastly refused to admit into his earlier writing. Our main object in this study will be to track down the distinctive features which have emerged in each of the three writers, and in particular to ask whether their later work should cause us to modify some of the critical judgements that were made earlier in their careers.

Most people agree that, however good or bad a play it may have been, *Look Back in Anger* marked a turning-point in the post-war British theatre when it was presented at the Royal Court Theatre in May 1956. There is considerably more argument about the nature of the transformation that followed. In some writers' mythology, the late 1950s was a time when a basically bourgeois institution made a determined move to the left, and the theatre engaged itself with new-found commitment in radical social issues. To others, the important thing about the fifties was that theatre artists made a decisive break with naturalism to explore the darker, more irrational recesses of human nature using new theatrical techniques and an honesty that the polite language of drawing-room drama had never allowed. There are those, too, who believe that the theatre has revitalized itself by rediscovering its roots in popular entertainment. Elements of the performer's craft which had survived in the circus or the music-hall, but long been stifled by the literary orientations of the legitimate theatre, gradually regained their primacy in a theatre which had cast aside its spurious pretensions to respectability.

But one has only to glance at the history of the European and American theatre in the modern period, with its distinguished roll-call including Jarry, Meyerhold, Brecht, Cocteau and O'Neill, not to mention Artaud, to see that there is nothing very novel about the break with naturalism or the development of political or popular theatre. The revolution in the English theatre of the past twenty years or so has not been a once-and-for-all phenomenon, but belongs to a series of advances and retreats in the drama, and more particularly in the great modern movement which began in Europe towards the end of the last century.

There is another reason, too, why we should be cautious of attaching labels and distributing categories among the products of the post-war British theatre: in art, as in most branches of life, the British are empiricists who create first and theorize later, if at all. Few of the directors or writers of the period have produced work which can be neatly pigeon-holed, and in the end it is diversity and a lack of any discernible school of writing or theatrical approach that characterizes the period we are considering. Osborne, Arden and Pinter have been chosen to represent the contemporary English theatre in this study not simply because (with the possible addition of Arnold Wesker) they are the most substantial dramatists of their generation, but also because a comparison of their achievements illustrates the diversity as well as the strength of the postwar theatre.

In the following three chapters, each of the dramatists will be considered in turn: in this chapter I wish to approach the work of all three by way of some general remarks about the nature of dramatic criticism. Dramatic criticism, of course, falls into two fairly distinct categories. First of all there are the reviewers who contribute to newspapers, weeklies and journals. Their raw material is the play in performance; because of the conditions under which they work their contribution to knowledge is short and often hurried. As well as passing judgement upon a play and its performance, a good review contains a large descriptive element: a prospective theatregoer is interested in what a new play is about, what makes X's performance as Hamlet different from anyone else's, as much as he is in the critic's opinion as to whether it was good or bad. Naturally, since the critics can influence box office receipts, they are alternately flattered and reviled by the theatrical profession. Unfavourable reviews wound deeply, and a column inch of praise causes pleasure even when it comes from someone whose opinions you would otherwise distrust: the words 'Harold Hobson liked it' could be used as an acting exercise, so many conflicting emotions have they been known to convey. For my part, whatever the deficiencies of contemporary dramatic criticism may be, nothing can diminish my admiration for the facility with which the best reviewers can convey to the reader, in a paragraph or two, *what it was like* to have been at a performance.

The second approach is that of the critic writing an article or a book; although he is, one hopes, a theatregoer, he will be developing his analysis from the published text of a play and the merits of any one individual performance will be of less concern to him. His judgements will be developed at greater length and he is not forced to rush into print with instant opinion. This is no guarantee that he will be any wiser than the first-night critic, but ideally there should be an element of mature reflection in his work which the reviewer, jotting furtive notes in the stalls or the circle bar, can never hope to achieve. It is with this second kind that we are concerned here.

Things have improved over the years, but all too often works which are written to be performed are still analysed as if they were written to be read in the seclusion of one's home. One reason for this, I think, is that the nature of dramatic criticism (from now on I shall use that term to refer to the study and interpretation of plays) has not been sufficiently explored; and in particular the differences between it and literary criticism need further investigation. Whereas a literary critic has to deal with a finished product in print before him, the dramatic critic has to conjure up in his mind's eye, and conjure up for his readers, a three-dimensional picture of which the words on the page before him are only a flimsy part. If the critic's job is to evoke, analyse and finally to evaluate our response to a work of art, the dramatic critic has to remember that he can only refer obliquely to the work he is considering. A printed text is not a performance; a performance is only one of many alternative interpretations of a written text.

Before dramatic criticism comes to sound so daunting a task that only the foolhardy will ever attempt it, we should remember that one writer who contributed as much as anyone in this century to the study of theatrical literature, Harley Granville-Barker, was sufficiently modest to call his contributions *Prefaces to Shakespeare*. All dramatic criticism is in fact in the nature of a preface rather than a definitive interpretation. A factual knowledge of the kind of theatre for which a dramatist wrote (or is writing) can provide insights of one sort; a study of the text as language written for delivery by a company of actors can tell you something else; an analysis of the structure of the play in terms of theatrical climaxes and visual imagery will reveal some of its non-literary qualities; and finally, a knowledge of the psychology of the actor–audience relationship applied to an individual text may help to explain its effect in theoretical terms. Synthesize all this, and a little else besides, and you may have a valuable study of a play; the interpretation of it will only be complete when a director and his team of actors contribute their insights as well. The dramatic critic, in other words, must reconcile himself to devoting a wide variety of techniques to somewhat more limited ends than those of the pure literary critic. His compensating reward, as it is for all those who work in and around the theatre, is that he is contributing something to a cooperative, living artistic venture.

Any writer who sets out his thoughts on the nature of criticism runs the risk that from then on the few modest points he may be trying to make will be dismissed as a failure to fulfil the promise of his own programme. So let me make it clear that I am far from putting forward the following chapters as exemplary specimens of dramatic criticism. In my study of the three authors concerned I shall be less concerned with general rules than with highlighting their individual qualities. There is, however, one question related to the nature of dramatic criticism which I do wish to explore more fully in the work of our three dramatists, namely the creation of dramatic character: because here, I think, lies one of the deeper and more misunderstood problems of dramatic criticism.

If a market research firm were commissioned to discover public opinion on what people look for in dramatists instead of in washing machines or motor cars, it is very likely that 'creation of character' would come near the top of the list. The dramatist writes for actors, and actors must create a character and present it in such a way as to impress and convince an audience. Most people, asked to search their memories for their most cherished theatrical experiences, will recall occasions when the work of playwright and actor have fused together so that character, emotion and situation are for a moment perfectly conveyed through speech and action.

So the man in the street (or, if you like, the girl in the gallery) can hardly be blamed for assuming that the dramatist is, above all, a man who puts characters on to the stage. Not all the experts have agreed. Aristotle, for instance, placed plot above character, which puzzles many of his readers today and indeed may have been unusual in his own day, since he felt obliged to argue the point at some length. But when we recall that by 'plot' Aristotle meant, not simply an invented story (most Greek tragedies took their outlines from a familiar myth in any case) but 'the ordering of the incidents'[1] we can see that it was really dramatic *structure*, the way a play is put together, that the ancient philosopher rated so highly.

One reason, perhaps, why so much more emphasis is commonly placed on character is that the structure of a play, except in the work of exceptionally pioneering dramatists, has a good deal that is conventional about it, while it is in the portrayal of character that a writer's individuality seems to come out. We can all supply our own examples, from Shakespeare's Hamlet to Chekhov's three sisters, of characters who seem to express all that is uniquely personal in their authors' theatre. We are less likely to say that naturalism, or a new use of the soliloquy, or the handling of exposition scenes is a contribution to our spiritual experience in quite the same way.

Because characterization is so obviously the personal domain of the dramatist a number of people, including some distinguished literary critics as well as our man in the street and girl in the gallery, commit one of their major errors in approaching the work of a dramatist. The mistake is to assume that the analysis of a play is essentially an analysis of the characters in that play. In fact, this approach is not merely superficial; in some cases it can positively mislead.

For one thing, structural conventions are no mere historical peculiarities which can somehow be placed in a separate compartment from the dramatist's lasting and universal qualities. The Chorus in Greek tragedy, for instance, is not simply a remainder from some archaic form of ritual drama; if we ignore it we miss important elements of the dramatist's religious thinking, and if we miss *that* we shall not be very successful in making sense of the characters' actions. The large sweep of the action in Elizabethan tragedy looks back to the mystery cycles of the Middle Ages, and this in turn tells us something of the cosmic importance of the figures who strut the stage of tragedy. Even Naturalism itself, regarded by its supporters as a form of drama where no tricks of rhetoric or artificialities of plot stand between the audience and the dramatist's characters, has its own favourite structural devices, not a few of which embody assumptions about the nature of man and society[2].

And Naturalism, which became the dominant mode of dramatic writing towards the end of the last century, has been under attack almost since its inception from a succession of rival Isms—Symbolism, Expressionism, Futurism, Constructivism, Absurdism—all of them related to wider literary or artistic movements and, so far as the theatre is concerned, calling for new and revolutionary approaches to the relationship between character and action as represented on the stage.

In short, if we read a play (or, for that matter, direct it or act in it) as if its historical background were only of importance to the wardrobe mistress, we shall probably miss a good deal of the author's distinctive qualities. No director, one hopes, would set out to recreate as it were archaeologically the exact conditions under which a play was originally staged, but he would be failing in his duty if he did not attempt to guide his actors into some coherent way of relating the various dramatic devices employed by the author to their own portrayals of the characters they represent. For the actor it is summed up in one word—style—succinctly defined by Sir John Gielgud as 'knowing what sort of a play you're in'.

There is another, much more fundamental and perhaps less obvious point to be made. It is easy to assume that 'character' means the same thing to all men. Nothing could be further from the truth. It may be that human nature never changes, but it would be difficult to find two men, and in particular two dramatists, who could agree upon a definition of human nature. Although, as I have suggested, most of us assume that the dramatist is concerned with the portrayal of character, or of action through character, at a deeper level he is concerned with the nature of the human condition itself. It is here that the peculiar nature of the dramatic art presents the most subtle problems to actors and directors and to critics and scholars. Speech and action, the stuff of drama, are the outward signs of character, but each dramatist uses a different code, so to speak, to relate these signs to the forces that make his individuals what they are. We can trace this across history: the difference between Shakespearian and Restoration Comedy, for instance, is not simply a matter of dramatic conventions and staging conditions, but involves two very different views of human nature, in particular of the relationship between the sexes and the role of that relationship inside society. But we can trace it within a single period as well: the contrast between Shakespearian and Jonsonian comedy provides an obvious example.

So far as our own century is concerned, one has only to think of two of the major intellectual forces to have shaped our thinking, Karl Marx who believed that individual consciousness is a product of class and society, and Sigmund Freud who argued that our adult personalities are shaped by infantile sexual experience, to be made aware of the wide range of approaches to character open to the dramatist. The dramatist (if he is any good) does not need to announce 'I am a Marxist' or 'My treatment of character is influenced by R D Laing' in the programme; nor do his characters give obvious clues about the nature of the author's beliefs the moment the curtain rises. It is a more subtle matter of relating speech to action, of watching patterns of action emerge as the play proceeds, of tracking down the significance of the relationship between individual characters. The actor, like a chameleon who changes his colour to suit his environment, must move instinctively from one view of human nature to the next as he represents characters in plays by different authors; those of us who are not actors and set ourselves the task of analysing the difference between one dramatist and another, find ourselves falling back on the wisdom of Aristotle and agreeing that character is essentially subordinate to 'plot' or, to put it another way, 'the ordering of the incidents' will tell us more than anything else about the distinctive features of a play.

This is perhaps as far as general argument can take us; let us now see what a look at three specific plays can tell us about this relationship between character, action and that elusive quarry, the author's world-picture. There can be no doubt that the characters created for the stage by Osborne, Pinter and Arden could hardly differ more from one another; we are seeking to define rather than to discover what it is that sets them apart. The backgrounds chosen by the three playwrights have not had much in common since those early days when *Look Back in Anger*, *Live Like Pigs* and *The Birthday Party* took a hard look at the seedy side of life; but for the purpose of comparison I have chosen three plays written in the mid-sixties, when each of the authors had established a reputation and something of a characteristic style, on the grounds that each of the three is set in an office where professional men and women, under varying degrees of tension, go about their everyday business. One of the plays, Osborne's *Inadmissible Evidence*, was written for the stage and is generally regarded as one of its author's major achievements; both of the others, Pinter's *Tea Party* and Arden's *Wet Fish* (surely the most unattractive title ever to have flickered on to the box) are television plays, neither of which has equalled *Inadmissible Evidence* in critical esteem. The two television plays take advantage of the medium's flexibility to cut quickly from scenes in the office to scenes in the outer world, while *Inadmissible Evidence* observes the unities of time and place with almost classical severity. When all these differences are allowed for, enough points of comparison remain to allow us, I hope, to draw some interesting conclusions.

The world of the office has its own mythology: the ringing telephones, the arcane jargon of the business world, the endless cups of tea, the office Casanova and the bombshell in the typing pool. It has also its symbolic aspects as a kind of meta-world which mirrors the crises, conflicts and emotional upheavals of life outside in a nine-to-five pattern of rivalry, friendship and fragile decorum among the desks and filing cabinets. Out of this raw material come three very different plays.

John Arden sub-titled *Wet Fish* 'A Professional Reminiscence for Television' and called it 'a fictional version of one of my own experiences during the two years I spent as an inefficient assistant in an architect's office'. He asks the reader to accept it as a 'straight situation comedy' written 'deliberately in a flat and naturalistic manner'[3]; one might expect to find it, therefore, a play without the characteristics of Arden's drama at its most idiosyncratic. Up to a point, it is so. The use of verse to punctuate the action, for instance, normally a hall-mark of Arden's work, is limited to little more than a few stanzas of a ditty with the attractive opening phrase 'When father papered the parlour'. But dramatists, like other artists, work by minute touches as much as by broad effects, and the recurring snatches of the ditty, from the moment we first hear it being whistled 'loudly and out of tune' as the camera picks out the architect's drawing office in the opening sequence, to the soulful words of the Polish *emigré* much later, all fall into a pattern which suggests that the 'deliberate naturalism' of this piece is not quite so straightforward as it appears.

We have Arden's word for it that the play draws on his own youthful experience, and indeed much of the dialogue with its talk of specifications, variation orders and eighth-circle bend-sections, betrays that bemused fascination with professional slang which often overtakes writers looking back on their earlier occupations. But a moment's reflection will tell us that the reasons for choosing an architect's office as the setting may not have been entirely autobiographical. Unlike the solicitor in *Inadmissible Evidence* or the marketer of sanitary ware in *Tea Party*, the architect belongs to a profession which literally shapes the homes and cities we live in. That famous 'quality of life' can be enhanced or utterly ruined by the designs issued from the architect's drawing-board. It would be no surprise, therefore, to find a degree of social awareness creeping into the text. This indeed proves the case, but as so frequently where Arden is concerned, not quite in the way we should expect.

The opening scene, which presents the three assistants bent over their drawing boards, quickly establishes them as office 'types'; with dramatic economy, their characters are immediately made evident in the way they react to a phone that rings insistently. 'Oh bother the thing!' cries Ruth nervously, as she smudges her drawing. Leslie, the cheerful rebel, is less concerned: 'It's only half past nine. Never take phone calls before tea-break.' Peter, the conscientious, ever reliable worker, simply says 'I'm busy'. Krank, the fourth member of the team, is represented—equally characteristically—by a deserted drawing-board. There is nothing particularly subtle in this opening; indeed there is something rather obvious about the instant characterization. As the play proceeds it becomes clear that Ruth and the absent Krank are more important to the action than the other two, but it is fair to say of the three actors we have seen so far that we never learn a great deal more about their personalities than is given us in those opening lines. If we want to know something of their family lives, how they come to be in this office, what they do when they go home at night, we shall be disappointed; in fact, despite the avowed naturalism of this play, there is a lack of breadth to the characters which almost amounts to caricature.

One by one we are introduced to the remaining characters: Garnish, the ambitious head of the firm; Treddlehoyle, long ago his first customer and now seeking some alterations to his fish shop; assorted customers of Treddlehoyle; representatives of the various crafts and businesses associated with the builder's trade; the inevitable tea-man. Gradually, a picture of life in the architects' office and its ramifications is built up, and that picture becomes quite complex—more complex in fact than what we see of the characters involved. Apart from a few deft touches which give some extra flesh and blood to the mysterious Krank and the homely Treddlehoyle, the architects remain architects, the customers customers, the builder's men builder's men. Is this a criticism? Only if we are prepared to object to Arden's whole approach to the question of character and action. Every artist works by selection as much as invention, and we learn so little about certain aspects of Arden's dramatic characters not because he is less perceptive or imaginative than other writers, but because he prefers to shine the searchlight upon unusual corners of human activity. Arden is interested in public rather than private life.

As the play progresses it becomes evident that Treddlehoyle's innocent desire to protect his rheumatic joints from the elements by closing in his wet-fish department is tangled up with other matters. The building contract goes to Mr Barker of Durable Construction, whose brother has influence on the local council. (His tender was certainly the lowest, says Garnish emphatically: 'But a great deal depends upon which firms you ask to tender in the first place . . .')[4] The busy Garnish entrusts the work to Ruth; the inexperienced girl is easy game for the contractors, and she makes a thorough mess of her first assignment. To cap it all, the roof-timbers over Treddlehoyle's shop are found to be rotten, and in a surprise move (as the newspapers say) Krank, the Polish *emigré* whose telephone calls throughout the play have revealed his interest in a number of properties where the police keep a close eye on the ladies of the house, acts swiftly and buys the fish shop. Small wonder that the long-suffering Treddlehoyle finally confronts Garnish and accuses him of letting him down—at a moment that causes maximum embarassment, since Garnish was in the middle of an expensive lunch with the Archdeacon, negotiating the delicate question of the damage his excavations were causing to the local cathedral.

It is easy to imagine the moral of this tale: the small shopowner, representing decency and honest simplicity, is ignored by the impersonal dictates of commerce and exploited by petty crooks, all of which is symbolized in architectural terms by the erection of massive, ugly office blocks while the human values of the corner shop and the ancient cathedral are wantonly destroyed. Look a little more closely at *Wet Fish*, and you will find that Arden divides his sympathies rather differently. Garnish really means it when he says that 'in this business, you never try to pull a fast one over your client'. He is genuinely upset when he discovers Ruth's naive incompetence. She might easily have been the heroine (the simple innocent outwitted by small-minded profiteers); in fact she has fallen down on the job and deserves the rocket she gets from Garnish. We have heard so much of evil landlords that it is a surprise to find Krank a sympathetic character, whose devious schemes go with a gentle personality and a loathing of violence.

Arden's delineation of character *is* sharp, but in an unexpected way. He is a deeply moral writer, and *Wet Fish* is a portrait not so much of men at work as of the morality of provincial life at work (a subject tackled again, and more successfully, in *The Workhouse Donkey*). The characters are less interesting in themselves than as part of an interlocking community bound together by self-interest and ambition, but basically decent. Everyone, from the tea-man to the high-flying Garnish, observes a complicated system of rules which governs the favours they perform for each other, the returns they can expect, and (the most important aspect of any set of rules) the point beyond which one cannot go.

What seem at first sight to be the random events of life in the architect's office—phone calls from the Cathedral, details of the

Treddlehoyle conversion, complaints about the inefficiency of Durable Construction, the growing excitement about the lucrative Prince Consort Street scheme—are all marshalled as instances of the strategies and counter-strategies which operate in this interdependent community. We have seen that Arden labelled *Wet Fish* 'straight situation comedy'; in the classical tradition, situation comedy is sparked off by a surprise incident or arrival which unsettles a stable community; danger and disorder threaten and eventually harmony is restored. The minor disaster around which *Wet Fish* revolves occurs because the ingenuous Ruth does not yet realize how the game is played; the carefully contrived plot produces its crop of humorous situations, but each of them has a hard moral edge.

Wet Fish is a slight work, but it illustrates many of Arden's characteristics well. He enjoys investigating man as a social, political animal, and showing that our hard-and-fast moral certainties are too simple to apply to the complicated situations in which most of the business of the world is carried out. To that extent his plays often lead the audience's expectations astray: just when some fairly obvious dramatic effect might be expected to expose the villains or heroes in their true light, Arden reverses our sympathies. Most puzzling of all, the moral uncertainties of public life are undermined still further by the unpredictable vagaries of personal feeling. We have seen that there is much about his characters' private lives that Arden does not tell us, but this is because he selects and concentrates, and not because he is unaware of the dictates of the human heart. And romance does come unexpectedly to Ruth among the diseased rafters of Treddlehoyle's shop, when Krank appears, mysteriously as ever, through the connecting wall. We ought to be outraged, no doubt, at the thought of this shiftless racketeer taking advantage of a young, unhappy girl. In fact the incident is touching and Arden's sense of poetry, suppressed through most of this play, sets the seal on this union of innocence and experience when Krank sings softly (to the tune of 'When father papered the parlour'):

> Before I came from Poland,
> I filled a sack with earth:
> I wanted it shown,
> I needed it known,
> Wherever I went I'd still be at home.
> But they covered the road with barbed wire:
> It was all I could do to get through.
> My earth was scattered across the wind
> And my sack was torn in two. (p. 137)

Simply as titles, *Wet Fish* and *Tea Party* are so discordant that one hesitates before putting them in the same sentence. Likewise with the plays: Pinter seems to concentrate on aspects of human behaviour so remote from those of *Wet Fish* that they might belong to a different species. And treatment of character, as always, is bound up with a larger whole which affects language, structure and setting.

To begin with the setting: whereas the work of the architect impinges upon society at large, the manufacturer of sanitary ware finds himself in a less eminent position. His products are essential, and yet ludicrous. His

9

lavatory bowls should be kept out of sight in the smallest room; he displays them in shop windows. The contrast between his gleaming porcelain and the uses to which it is put encourages the least philosophical amongst us to a few random generalities about the continual assault from within to which human dignity is subject. The difference between the opening shots of *Tea Party*, as the camera ranges along 'a selection of individually designed wash basins, water closets and bidets, all lit by hooded spotlights' in the corridor of a richly-appointed office suite, and the young architects intent over their drawing boards in *Wet Fish*, is so obvious that it hardly needs comment.

In *Wet Fish* the plot follows the fortunes of some of the architects' plans as they leave the drawing board and come to fruition on their sites around the city. The opening image is linked to the play's structure in a clearly discernible way. This is not so in the case of Pinter's water closets and bidets. As has often been observed, the room which forms the setting in Pinter's early plays has an almost living relationship with the actors. It offers them a haven of security; it keeps out (or lets in) intruders from the mysterious, menacing world beyond. This relationship between setting and character is developed with varying degrees of complexity in the dramatist's later work, with *Tea Party* no exception. One cannot call Pinter's settings symbolic: a symbol points away from itself towards something else, and Pinter's work remains absolutely resistant to that sort of interpretation. At the same time if you are to call them realistic (as Pinter himself would undoubtedly insist that you should) you must use the term in a rather unusual sense, referring to some inner authenticity rather than to photographic exactitude.

Disson's occupation as a manufacturer of sanitary ware is neither completely arbitrary nor as self-evidently purposeful as the choice of an architect's office for *Wet Fish* or a solicitor's for *Inadmissible Evidence*. Rather it operates like some recurrent image in a poem, looming up every now and then with half-conscious mental associations which contribute directly or indirectly to the final effect.

If the setting in *Tea Party* does not yield anything like the same amount of information about the profession of its characters as *Wet Fish*, it becomes instead an extension of Disson's personality and the perturbations that afflict him. Although we are given no very clear idea of what precisely Disson does in his office, there is a great deal that we do learn. Consider this little exchange very near the opening of the play, when Disson interviews an applicant for a job:

DISSON: Oh yes. We manufacture more bidets than any one else in England. [*He laughs.*] It's almost by way of being a mission. Cantilever units, hidden cisterns, footpedals, you know, things like that.

WENDY: Footpedals?

DISSON: Instead of a chain or plug. A footpedal.

WENDY: Oh. How marvellous.

DISSON: They're growing more popular every day and rightly so. [*Wendy crosses her right leg over her left.*] Well now, this . . . post is, in fact, that of my personal assistant. Did you understand that? A very private secretary, in fact. And a good deal of responsibility would undoubtedly devolve upon you. Would you ... feel yourself capable of discharging it?

WENDY: Once I'd correlated all the fundamental features of the work, sir, I think so, yes.

DISSON: All the fundamental features, yes. Good. (p. 10)

If we were to divide this, Stanislavsky style, into text and sub-text, the text would be clear to the point of occasional vacuity, the sub-text packed with interesting implications. The normal situation seems to be reversed, and while the applicant for the job appears cool and self-possessed, the interviewer shows signs of unease. Wendy has to make no real attempt to establish her qualifications for the job; instead it is Disson who is driven into boasting about his prowess in his unenviable profession. The momentary hesitation as he mentions 'this ... post' sets up more than one suggestion. Disson's need for a 'personal assistant' has something unusual about it; we suspect that some secret need may be asserting itself. And Disson's apparent confusion after Wendy has crossed her legs makes it fairly clear that this is a moment in which sexual attraction is busy at its work of breaking down the norms, reversing the roles, and making weak the strong.

Pinter's plots contain many puzzles, but there can be no doubt as to the closely-textured structure of his work. In this passage of dialogue we can detect themes which are to emerge time after time, with growing urgency, throughout the play. Disson's sense of insecurity, suggested rather than emphasized at this stage, is repeated so often that his life, at home and in the office, can almost be interpreted as a perpetual quest for reassurance—about his strength as a boss, as a father, as a lover. The hint of a loss of self-control on Disson's part as Wendy crosses her legs is a foretaste of the bizarre developments that are to affect Disson's character as the play progresses.

'I'm ... getting married tomorrow' reveals Disson (with another of those hesitations) shortly after he has offered Wendy the job. 'Yes, this is quite a good week for me, what with one thing and another.' With this off-hand introduction of the question of marriage, so soon after the obvious excitement caused by Wendy's arrival, the scene is set for the twin forces which are to destroy Disson's slender hold over himself.

Disson's marital misfortunes begin with the last-minute defection of his best man, so that toast to the groom (all-important, for some reason, to Disson) is delivered by his prospective brother-in-law, a man of recent acquaintance who deflects the speech away from Disson's virtues to dwell at length upon his sister's qualities:

Now he has married a girl who equals, if not surpasses, his own austere standards of integrity. He has married my sister, who possesses within her that rare and uncommon attribute known as inner beauty, not to mention the loveliness of her exterior.

(pp. 14–15)

All of which is a little unfair, for it was the same brother-in-law Willy who had just delivered the toast to the bride:

I remember the days my sister and I used to swim together in the lake at Sunderley. The grace of her crawl, even then, as a young girl. I can remember those long summer evenings at Sunderley, my

11

> mother and I crossing the lawn towards the terrace and through
> the great windows hearing my sister play Brahms.   (p. 14)

There is comedy, of course, in this parody of a wedding speech, but a
touch of the sinister too as Willy reminisces (how truthfully the audience
has no means of knowing) about the graceful childhood of the girl who is
getting married. Jealousy of another person's past can be aroused almost
as easily as jealousy of an old friendship; it is an experience from which
one is excluded. There is scarcely a Pinter character who does not at
some stage recall the past—to assert his identity, or as a gesture of
friendship, or as an act of hostility.

Disson reacts strangely, suddenly offering his new brother-in-law a
post in his firm; Willy accepts with alacrity. Is he consciously mounting
an assault upon Disson's supremacy, undermining his confidence and inveigling himself into the office, or has he been innocently motivated in a
series of actions which are to rebound upon Disson only because of his
own distorted sense of persecution? Most authors would give us a few
clues; Pinter leaves it to us to interpret the evidence as we please. But the
evidence is superbly presented. Here is Disson addressing Willy on his
first day at the office:

> Now, dependence isn't a word I would use lightly, but I will use it
> and I don't regard it as a weakness. To understand the meaning of
> the term dependence is to understand that one's powers are limited
> and that to live with others is not only sensible but the only way
> work can be done and dignity achieved. Nothing is more sterile or
> lamentable than the man content to live within himself.   (p. 19)

Much later in the play, as it works towards its climax, Willy, Disson and
his wife are having an uneasy evening at home. Willy reminisces again,
with Disson trying desperately to share the memories:

> WILLY: Music playing.
> DISSON: On the piano.
> WILLY: The summer nights. The wild swans.
> DISSON: What swans? What bloody swans?   (p. 40)

The exchange continues, getting odder and odder, until Diana cuts it
short by saying 'Come to bed'—one of those sudden sexual invitations
that Pinter's women are prone to make. 'You can say that, in front of
him?', responds Disson, and what seems to be boiling up to a violent
quarrel ends only when Disson invites Willy into a partnership in the
firm. Memories from which Disson is excluded, a feeling that Willy is
closer to his sister than he the husband, tension relieved by a gesture of
friendliness (or is it defeat?) by Disson; the pattern of this scene is
almost identical to that of the wedding scene, but now Disson is nearer
to breaking point, and between it has come his confident pep-talk to
Willy about the virtues of dependence, as significant and packed with
irony as a hero's display of pride in classical tragedy.

The same psychological forces which bedevil Disson's relations with
Willy are at work undermining his parental confidence. He is already the
father of two bumptious twins, who were 'very young' when their
mother died[5]. The twins, miniature monsters old enough to challenge
their father's supremacy at everything from table tennis to woodwork,
are walking definitions of the military offence of 'dumb insolence' and

constitute yet one more threat to Disson's beleaguered sensibilities. The essence of the plot, however, is concentrated in Disson's relationship with the two women, wife and secretary.

Nowhere I suppose is the gap between the words we use and the experiences we undergo so wide as in our sexual lives, and sex turns us all into Pinter characters, muttering trite inconsequentialities as profound, irrational mysteries engulf us. It is hardly surprising that the physical presence of Wendy, cool, proper and yet sometimes, it seems, ready for more intimate approaches, unsettles and finally overpowers her newly-married boss.

Since so much is left unexplained in *Tea Party*, as in all of Pinter's work, rational explanation of the characters' behaviour-patterns is often wide of the mark, and it is far more important for the critic and reader to pin-point the dramatic climaxes of the play. There can be no doubt that, although it occurs in a relatively quiet scene, the turning point in Disson's career comes dramatically when he agrees to let his wife work in the office alongside her brother, 'to be closer to you', as Willy explains[6]. Now neither the office nor the home can offer security to Disson: Willy and Diana, united by their mysterious sibling bond, pursue him from one haven to the other, teaming up with allies—the twins at home, Wendy in the office—in either territory. Disson's isolation and waning prowess is signalled by a physical disability—sudden moments of sightlessness marked in the original production (rather ineffectively, if my memory of nine years ago is reliable) by the screen going blank. An optician finds nothing wrong with his eyes, but he falls into the strange habit in the office of bandaging his eyes with a chiffon scarf of Wendy's: blindness is a condition of total dependence which in this context immediately takes on sexual connotations. 'I always feel like kissing you when you've got that on round your eyes', says Wendy. 'Do you know that? Because you're all in the dark.' 'No' she says a moment later, 'you mustn't touch me, if you're not wearing your chiffon.'[7] The contradictory aspect of a sexual relationship, attraction and repulsion, are polarized by Disson's retreat into childlike helplessness and Wendy's reactions to him in and out of that condition.

The tea party of the title is organized in the office to celebrate the first wedding anniversary. Everyone is there: Disson's parents, old characters uttering perfunctory Pinterisms and a far cry from the magnificent parental couple dreamed up by Willy; the twins; Disley, the defaulting best man; and of course the unholy alliance of Willy, Diana and Wendy. What should be a successful businessman's triumph, a celebration of success in public and private life, ends up as the scene of Disson's breakdown. While he sits there with eyes bandaged, listening to the rattle of tea cups and the whisper of conversation, he suffers a mental picture of Willy and the two girls playing lovers' games among the office furniture—all in his mind's eye, as the camera angles lead us to suspect, but enough of a final nightmare to drive Disson (his bandage finally removed) to one of those staring, speechless silences which form the chilling conclusion to so many of Pinter's plays.

Whereas Arden, for his purposes, saw character in terms of social function and social relationships, Pinter sees it largely as a field of powerful, inexplicable forces acting from within. Arden builds up a genuine interest in the projects his architects are engaged upon—naturally enough since this is so closely allied to their social role. For Pinter the office setting provides an open-ended opportunity for a variety of dramatic images: the boss's interview becomes an archetypal conflict between masculine power and feminine subtlety; the arrival of Willy and Diana expresses Disson's decline and fall in territorial terms; his enthusiasm for the gleaming sanitary ware he sells is linked obliquely to the grotesque sexual fantasies which end by turning his office into a nightmare.

> *The location where a dream takes place. A site of helplessness, of oppression and polemic. The structure of this particular dream is the bones and dead objects of a Solicitor's Office. It has a desk, files, papers, dust, books, leather armchairs, a large, Victorian coat stand, and the skeleton of an outer office with clerks, girls and a telephonist. Downstage is a DOCK in which stands the prisoner of this dream, BILL MAITLAND.*

The words which introduce the text of *Inadmissible Evidence* dictate the convention of the play more directly than the bare, factual indications of either *Wet Fish* or *Tea Party*. Furthermore, they are far from gracefully written. In both respects they are characteristic of Osborne's stage directions, indicating that uneasy relationship with naturalism which marks his dramatic career. A new attempt to break away from picture-frame illusion began in earnest on the English stage shortly after *Look Back in Anger*, and this is reflected in much of Osborne's work from *The Entertainer* onwards, until in many of his mature works he returns like a prodigal after a misspent youth to the naturalism he could never entirely reject. *Inadmissible Evidence* occupies a kind of half-way house. The hectoring tone of the opening stage direction, and some subsequent passages, insist that we should look on the action not as reality so much as some kind of hallucinatory reconstruction of events inside the hero's increasingly muddled and desperate head; we have only to listen to a few snatches of dialogue, as convincing as an overheard conversation, to realize that the quality of the play exists quite independently of its structural devices.

In the two plays we have just considered the dramatists seem to have left out about as much as they have put in. The architects' home lives and Disson's office routines are pretty callously neglected, and although it is possible to show that there are sound artistic reasons for this, nevertheless some explaining is necessary to that hypothetical man in the street who believes that creation of character *per se* is the primary function of the dramatist. In *Inadmissible Evidence*, on the other hand, we seem at last to have met with a play that presents us with a central character whose emotional response to a situation of crisis is presented with full-blooded attention to detail. Instead of the process of selection we have observed in Arden and Pinter, Osborne seems determined to let nothing stand between his characters and the audience. In the following passage Bill Maitland tries to settle down to a morning stint in the solicitor's office which he runs (Hudson, his chief clerk, has just made a half-hearted protest against Bill's interest in the shapely new switchboard operator—evidently a perennial problem in this office):

14

Right. No Joy. For the moment, anyway. Goes against the Rules.
Which is the best thing. Right: work, work. Mrs Garnsey. Where
are my pills? There should be some in here. Anyway, I always keep
three in reserve in my ticket pocket. Where the hell are they? Joy!
Wish I didn't drink so much. And I keep wanting to sleep. I finally
took a pill at four this morning, went off at five, then I couldn't get
up. I couldn't even move at first.

[Joy *appears*.]

I was all trussed up. My darling, have you seen my pills, my
headache pills?   (p. 32)

It is difficult to imagine either Arden or Pinter writing dialogue as closely
studded with realistic minutiae as this. Maitland's disintegrating hold
over his private and public life is there, down to the last detail—in the
search for his pills, the rueful admission that he is drinking too much and
not sleeping enough, the ineffectual determination to control his
wayward passion for Joy, not sustained even for the length of one speech,
and in the desperate attempts to get to grips with the case of Mrs
Garnsey.

Osborne is a dramatist who seems to catch character in a tone of voice.
More than with any other dramatist I know, reading the text is like
hearing the performance over again, so closely has Osborne linked
language to the volatile personalities of his dramatic characters to
produce superb, indelibly memorable performances from his actors; no-
one who saw Nicol Williamson in the part of Maitland is likely to forget
the experience. It would indeed be possible to write a great deal about
the 'character' of Bill Maitland, both in psychological terms and as an acting role full of challenge and opportunity. His hypochondria, his
womanizing, the barrage of sarcasm and invective that hides a burning
need for the assurance of human contact, and above all the passionate
egotism that forces us, willy-nilly, to see the world from his point of
view—all these elements are far more compelling that the rather
shadowy interviews he conducts with his clients or indeed the collapsing
relationships with his wife, his daughter, his lover and mistresses which
form the main thread of the plot. Indeed, if these elements were not compelling, there would be little to say about the play, since by far the largest
part of it consists of dialogue delivered by Maitland to one captive
auditor after another.

Can we say, then, that creation of character is all (or almost all) there is
to *Inadmissible Evidence*? Let us return to the point from which we
started, Osborne's description of the setting as 'the location where a
dream takes place' and the implications of this piece of stage-craft.

'William Henry Maitland, you are accused of having unlawfully
and wickedly published and made known, and caused to be
procured and made known, a wicked, bawdy and scandalous object
. . .'

The opening words of the play, solemnly delivered by a Clerk of the
Court who in the next scene turns out to be Maitland's own junior clerk,
set the tone of the play by directing all the attention upon Maitland. In
symbolic terms they point to some vaguely obscene act of which he is guilty, but in emotional terms the prisoner in the dock is bound to command

an element of sympathy, and this opening sequence has the effect not only of putting Maitland on trial before us, but also making us favour him, whatever his faults, against the impersonal forces which seem to be plotting his destruction. But this is far from being the only effect of the dream structure imposed upon the play. At the beginning of Act II, in another clumsily-written stage direction, Osborne notes:

> *This telephone conversation and the ones that follow it, and some of the duologues should progressively resemble the feeling of dream and unreality of* BILL'S *giving 'evidence' at the beginning of Act I. Some of the time it should all seem actually taking place at the particular moment, naturally, casual, lucid, unclouded. At others the grip of the dream grows tighter . . .* (p. 59)

Eventually, says Osborne, we must doubt whether 'there is anyone to speak to at all'.

The disintegration of Maitland's personality, in other words, is echoed in the play's structure by the growing confusion between reality and illusion. This immediately sets the monologues in the play in a fresh perspective. The clients, for instance, whose personal lives pass before Maitland as he discusses their petitions for divorce, are less representations of genuine people than they are figments of Maitland's haunted imagination. The coincidence that their experience matches his so closely ('I know that nothing really works for him', says Mrs Garnsey of her husband: 'Not at the office, not his friends, not even his girls')[8] might be clumsy and inelegant were it not that the audience is being asked to share moments in Maitland's experience, common to those whose minds are at breaking point, when everyday events take on monumental significance and it seems that every chance encounter is part of a conspiracy to expose one's own raw suffering. Even that curious but touching long scene in which a homosexual client tells Maitland of the failure of his marriage and the discovery of his true sexual appetite, reveals some unexpected sympathies in Maitland's character and throws a little light upon the quest for hidden experience hinted at in the obscure charges of the trial scene.

Although it was suggested earlier that the play's quality might be independent of Osborne's suggestion that the action is in the nature of a dream, it may be conceded that nevertheless the author has nudged the audience closer to his hero's phobias and hallucinations by making them share these to some extent themselves. However, this is not the major element in the play and neither so original nor so prominent as Osborne's stage directions seem to suggest we should consider it. The opening sequence, and the later stage directions, could be removed and the portrait of Maitland's character would remain virtually undiminished.

Inadmissible Evidence is the study of an individual at a point of crisis and collapse. It has the structure always associated with tragedy: a solitary figure is slowly destroyed by the failings of the past as they come to light in the present. By the end Maitland's business is in ruins, he seems to be permanently estranged from his daughter and his wife, and his current lover visits him only to pay him an intensely painful farewell. A tragic hero should elicit our sympathy while at the same time accepting responsibility for a disaster he brings on his own head. In a peculiarly modern way, I think that Maitland fulfils these requirements. A true Osborne character, he has a paradoxical element about him. He is rude, domineering, arrogant and self-centred: and yet he wins our respect. Why? Maitland himself supplies the answer in a central scene where he harangues his teenage daughter, a speech full of distorted, incoherent rage and love:

> ... I still don't think what you're doing will ever, ever, ever, ever approach the fibbing, mumping, pinched little worm of energy eating away in this me, of mine, I mean. That is: which is that of being slowly munched and then diminished altogether. That worm, thank heaven, is not in your little cherry rose. You are un-selfconscious, which I am not. You are without guilt, which I am not ...
> (pp. 105–106)

It is that 'little worm of energy', with its associated consciousness of self and of human responsibility, which lifts Maitland above the common run of humanity and gives us different norms to judge him by. Whatever else, Maitland is not a petty person.

There is one view of tragedy which sees it entirely as an art-form centred on the human emotions: we witness, and share, the suffering of an individual. Another view of tragedy insists that in its highest form it has wider reverberations. In the twentieth century, social tragedy has depicted man as a victim of historical forces: it is necessary to ask whether Maitland's significance for an audience lies solely in his lacerating personality, or is linked somehow to a critical view of the society in which he finds himself. Here again we may find, perhaps, that Osborne's avowed intentions are not identical with the final achievement of the play.

In the opening 'dream sequence' it is clear that, among other things, Osborne is trying to set his hero in a context wider than the purely personal. Asked to take the oath, Maitland affirms:

> By my belief. My belief in ... in ... the technological revolution, the pressing, growing, pressing, urgent need for more and more scientists, and more scientists, for more and more ... schools and universities and universities and schools ...
> (p. 10)

So it goes on. It is only gradually that Maitland passes from these confused generalities to some understanding of his own situation: it is almost as if we see him building himself up and putting himself together from the inadequate odds and ends of fashionable contemporary belief. *Inadmissible Evidence* alarmed many critics, who thought that they saw a left-wing dramatist forking sharply to the right; the passage just quoted is implicitly critical of the dogmas closest to the progressive's heart. Whenever Maitland's diatribes move away from purely personal matters the jibes are all against the young, the liberal, the underprivileged. Some of Osborne's most memorable invective in *Inadmissible Evidence* is directed against the very causes he might have been expected to espouse, and the very people who might have supported him. Maitland is full of contempt for the masses, for trendy professional couples like his wife's friends who offered their guests dinner off 'wooden bowls, yes, sort of *Sunday Times* Supplement Primitive ... *very* badly cooked', not to mention for academics: 'He's probably the only man living', declares Maitland of his lover's donnish father, 'whose unconscious desires are entirely impersonal'. But the bitterest remarks are reserved for those folk-heroes of the swinging sixties, the generation who have 'all that youth everyone's so mad about and admires'. His daughter, he says, is 'sure to marry an emergent African ... That is, if she hasn't already sent her virginity to OXFAM.'[9] This theme reaches a harsh crescendo in Maitland's confrontation with his daughter:

> Of course, you are stuffed full of paltry relief for emergent countries, and marches and boycotts and rallies, you, you kink your innocent way along tirelessly to all that poetry and endless jazz and folk workship, *and* looking gay and touching and stylish all at the same time. But there isn't much loving in any of your kindnesses, Jane, not much kindness, not even cruelty, really, in any of you, not much craving for the harm of others ... (p. 106)

It is scarcely surprising that a general impression was formed that the original angry young man had abandoned the causes he was the first to champion on the stage, and as his own youth waned a sour and reactionary envy of the up-and-coming generation had set in. If we were to look on *Inadmissible Evidence* as a play with a primarily political or social basis this would clearly be a point of substance, and the best we could do would be to interpret Maitland as the spokesman of some desperate rearguard action, fighting for obscure but individual values in a world suffocating from mass-produced, artificial concern for good causes and enlightened modern living. But this would be to commit the error, almost as old as the theatre itself, of interpreting the words put into the mouth of one character as the 'message' of the play. Whenever they are, it is almost certainly a poor play, and *Inadmissible Evidence* is certainly a great deal more than a collection of impatient comments upon the way society is going. Just as Osborne attributes an artistic structure to his play which is only partially carried through, so too he seems to try to impose a social significance upon his work which is not really there. It is worth noting that of the passages quoted in the last two pages, the opening speech from the nightmare trial is pretentiously uninspired and unimpressive, while the latter witticisms are examples of satire at its explosive best.

As a general commentator upon modern society Osborne is unoriginal and often muddled; his genius lies in looking at society through the eyes of one sharply authentic individual, and using that view of society to sharpen and clarify dramatic character. *Inadmissible Evidence* is unmistakably a play of the mid-sixties; Maitland is caught up in the aftermath of the angry fifties as inextricably as he is with his lover and his daughter. But—however much they may reflect Osborne's own views—his diatribes possess artistic validity far more as an expression of his character than as political comment. In this respect Osborne's central character is almost exactly the reverse of the heroes of *Wet Fish*. They derive their interest from the way their private inclinations impinge upon the life of the community; public events and attitudes in *Inadmissible Evidence* are much more in the nature of material upon which Bill Maitland's overweening ego feeds itself. The difference between Maitland and the characters of *Tea Party* is perhaps more subtle. Personal relationships and their psychological undercurrents are important to both writers; but Pinter is concerned with stripping off the inessentials to portray the raw, archetypal conflicts that lurk unseen behind everyday exchanges, while Osborne creates a character who is unique in time, place and situation. Despite the author's apparent attempts to build Maitland into a central figure for our age it is his individuality, dramatically expressed in fiery language and scenes of high emotion, that survives to give the play its quality.

However, we must beware of thinking that Osborne is a kind of primitive among artists, using a rough-and-ready naturalism and a not-too-deep view of the world as a vehicle for his towering portraits of human character. Osborne at his best is a master of language, and that mastery implies a certain care about structure and form; but the form emerges through the language rather than through the action or the theatrical conventions employed.

If we return to Maitland's speech, already quoted, as he settles down to work in the morning we can say a great deal more about it if we respond to it, not simply as some stream-of-consciousness put into Maitland's mouth by Osborne, but as part of a carefully organized piece of dramatic language taking up themes and phrases which are introduced earlier and echoed time after time in the play. The headache pills, for instance, appear first in the trial scene, as Maitland pleads for indulgence from the judge: 'I can't, I'm sorry, I can't find my pills. I always have three or so in my ticket pocket. So sorry.'[10] At the beginning of Act II, when the morning light reveals Maitland sleeping on the office sofa, his crucial day begins with a quest for the headache pills and a glass of water. Mrs Garnsey's name recurs time after time, and the threat of her appearance hangs over Maitland's head throughout the first act. His faltering grip upon the world around is symbolized by the failure of his interview with her. Taxis no longer stop for Maitland, the influential barrister will not come to the phone for him, and the doleful Mrs Garnsey is a minor instance of his waning potency, coming back to haunt him in the second act as he talks of the party guests who would have ignored him if his wife had not been there:

> They would have passed me by like a blank hoarding or a tombstone, or waste ground by the railway line or something. . . . And then there was Mrs Garnsey . . . Mrs Garnsey, you remember her . . . I don't know what to do about her. . . .   (p. 62)

In big things as in small, the themes and patterns in Bill Maitland's dialogue carry the play forward. In the trial scene, as he attempts to identify himself before the judge, he plunges into a speech which is part self-justification and part an attempt to pin down his own identity, that sets the tone for the whole play:

> Perhaps I did think I might land up on the bench even. Or with learned counsel. Mr Jones. No, but I never seriously thought of myself being brilliant enough to sit in that company, with those men, among any of them with their fresh complexions from their playing fields and all that, with their ringing, effortless voice production and their quiet chambers, and tailors and mess bills and Oxford Colleges and going to the opera . . .   (pp. 16–17)

Here Maitland is talking to the judge; but in waking life the judge is Hudson, his all-knowing senior clerk. And here is Bill in the office, keeping Hudson from his work:

> I've always managed to keep everything in place, in place enough to
> get on with it, do my work, enjoy things, enjoy other people, take an
> interest in all kinds of things. I've tried to read, not just my own
> subject. I keep trying and the circle seems to get smaller.   (p. 33)

This passionate self-enquiry, in a language that places Maitland exactly
in a certain social and intellectual bracket, is as much a central theme of
the play as the breakdown that accompanies it; and although it is temp-
ting to draw upon it as evidence for Osborne's social and political preoccupations, nevertheless it is his accuracy in filtering character through
the particularities of life, age and class which is the major achievement.

This brief consideration of language brings us back squarely to the
point at which we started, the use to which the three dramatists put the
office setting of their plays. Osborne is certainly the most naturalistic of
the three: his office is an office and not a territorial image or a metaphor
for society at large. But naturalism is not necessarily the most simple
form, and it has been shown that the language of *Inadmissible Evidence*
has been put together to provide a pattern of recurring themes and ideas,
threading their way in and out of the text to create some order and unity
in the whole. This of course is not merely an empty technical trick, but
the principal means of objectifying Maitland's experience. And the office
in which Maitland sees his life collapsing provides not only the scene, but
also the material and the imagery for his journey to destruction. The
opening trial scene may be unoriginal as a theatrical device, but the sur-
real lawcourt, with its dry legal mumbo-jumbo and confused
jurisprudence, takes shape out of the stuff of Maitland's working life. It
is no accident that some of his most important monologues are delivered
by telephone, an indispensible feature of the lawyer's office but also, with
its distant voices and impregnable silences, a symbol of Maitland's
fading contacts with the outside world.

Maitland's rhetoric could not exist outside the setting which Osborne
has devised for it, and where he does introduce anti-naturalistic devices,
in the trial scene and the 'dream' quality of certain scenes, it is to
strengthen the identity of image and experience in the central character
which is the most distinctive feature of the play. Thus, although at a
superficial level one can point to certain naiveties in the structure of
Inadmissible Evidence, at a deeper level one can detect that organic
relationship between form and content which is one of the marks of a
major artist.

Notes to Chapter 1

1 *Poetics*, Chapter 6; T. S. Dorsch's translation in *Aristotle, Horace, Longinus: Classical
   Literary Criticism* (Penguin Classics, 1965), p. 39
2 For a discussion of this point, see Raymond Williams, *Drama in Performance* (revised
   edition, 1968), Chapter 6
3 *Soldier, Soldier and other plays*, pp. 10–11
4 p. 100
5 p. 21
6 p. 20
7 p. 45
8 p. 55
9 pp. 66, 109
10 pp. 14–15

2 John Osborne: from anger to detachment

It is a commonplace that the present generation of English dramatists numbers a high proportion of writers whose careers began upon the stage; and naturally enough the experience they have gained there is reflected in the quality of their plays. This is true of writers as diverse as Charles Wood, Henry Livings and Harold Pinter; it is also true, incidentally, of John Whiting, whose ill-fated plays of the early 1950s were later to be recognized as forerunners of the revival of English dramatic writing; and John Osborne, whose *Look Back in Anger* can justifiably be claimed to have been a turning-point in English drama, is an example *par excellence* of what Michael Billington calls 'The Actor as Writer'[1]. He had been an actor for some eight years when *Look Back in Anger* appeared, playing in repertory up and down the country and from time to time running his own seasons as an actor–manager.

Billington, of course, is not the first critic to have drawn attention to this aspect of Osborne's stage-craft, but he goes beyond the obvious points and demonstrates convincingly that much of the experience communicated to an audience in his first plays is, thinly disguised, experience of a kind likely to have been picked up by a repertory actor in the early 1950s. Even the plot-structure, he notes, conforms fairly closely to the sort of play, superficially neat and with climaxes in all the right places, but leaving a few credibility gaps as well, that Osborne himself must have appeared in during his weekly engagements. But, more important than that, his central characters are all *actors*.

George Dillon and Archie Rice, indeed, are performers by profession, and Billington traces in illuminating detail the clues which suggest that Jimmy Porter 'belongs more to the theatre than he does to the sweet-stall business'. If we accept that argument, it turns out that the tirades of the angriest of all the angry young men reflect not so much a new political consciousness as 'the problems of an actor buried in the rut of a Midlands weekly rep in the '50s, knowing that he has a talent and energy that have so far gone unrecognized'.[2]

This of course is not the whole of *Look Back in Anger*; but it seems to me that we can uncover some pointers to the fundamental nature of Osborne the dramatist if we pause to consider some of the characteristic features which make an actor an interesting and unusual human being. When one of Osborne's characters talks about the theatre his words have the ring of truth, but it is the portrayal of a character type rather than the details of professional life which gives Osborne's work its distinctive quality. For acting is not simply a profession; it is, much more than most occupations, a way of life, and it produces (or, perhaps more accurately, attracts to its ranks) a very pronounced sort of character which might, for the sake of convenience, be called the 'actor type'. Not all actors, of course, possess all the characteristics of the actor type which I shall try to define: many of them, off-stage, are modest, unassuming individuals to whom one would be glad to lend one's lawn-mower. At the same time we must all know people who, although they have never appeared on the stage, clearly conform to the pattern I am describing.

By nature, the actor is someone who thrives on display. Events around him are automatically converted into material for egocentric demonstrations of emotion, so that it often appears that what happens to the rest of the world is only important so far as it affects him. Although he often holds strong opinions on a variety of subjects, his opinions are less important to him as a guide-line for his own conduct than as an opportunity for impressing others with a sparkling exhibition of rhetoric or invective. On one's first acquaintance with him an 'actor type' will seem to have a sharply defined character, but often this will dissolve into a collection of emotions, opinions and prejudices which for all their immediacy do not reveal the stamp of a consistent personality behind them.

An actor is a kind of exposed essence of human being. When he is on stage he steps into one role after another, and must be on intimate terms with the entire range of human emotions; when he takes off the greasepaint he lacks the protective personality that most of us carry around to shield our true nature from the prying eyes of the world; but the need to display and communicate passion which is his stock in trade is not something that can be left behind in the dressing-room along with the wigs and the make-up. The actor type is always in search of an audience: all in all he can prove an enthralling but wholly demanding companion, supremely arrogant and yet supremely vulnerable.

Of course the truth is that we are all of us secretly convinced that we are the centre of the universe, and that we have been given the major role in a gigantic drama in which no-one else, even among those tied to us by the closest links of friendship, family or love, shares our star billing. But most of us have learnt from hard experience that even if we play the star role in a drama of our own, we are mostly walk-ons in other people's scenarios, and we tend to keep our egos on a fairly tight lead accordingly. The glory of getting to know the actor type, on or off the stage, is that he draws us into a charmed circle where, secretly and vicariously, we can enjoy the outrageously self-centred, unashamedly emotional life which he leads. In this charmed circle we are listeners, watchers and sharers rather than part of the great outside world which feeds the actor type with his material. We are, in short, an audience, and the bond of emotional identification which exists between the actor and his audience is cemented by the complicity that links the actor type to a psychological hunger lurking within all of us.

Along with his centrally organized ego-system, the actor type often nourishes a strong vein of sexual ambivalence. Psychologists rarely tire of telling us that every human being is a blend of masculine and feminine qualities; but whereas most of us, even in this liberated age, tend to suppress the role for which nature has not physically equipped us, and do our best to carry on as gruff he-men or coy she-women, the actor (as Michael Billington points out in another revealing chapter of his book)[3] often spices his or her performance with a dash of bisexuality. 'Thank

22

God I'm normal', sings Archie Rice in *The Entertainer*, 'I'm just like the rest of you chaps.'[4] But hardly any of Osborne's protagonists can be said to be 'normal' in the conventional sense of the word. Only *A Patriot for Me* has homosexuality as its central subject, but one Osborne character after another betrays a fascination with the theme. Here, too, we may see the actor type opening up the secret world of self-indulgence for his audience, touching on forbidden sensibilities with a frankness which the restraints of everyday life forbid.

Osborne's interest in what I have called the actor type, together with the skill and diversity of his portraiture of it, goes a long way towards explaining his power and significance as a dramatist. His plays, rather like the characters who appear in them, get away with all sorts of outrageous deficiencies we ought by rights to condemn. Yet at the heart of them there lies a theatrical vitality which, however unfairly, makes much adverse criticism seem petty and pedantic.

In this brief description of the 'actor type', it may seem that my argument has suggested that such characters, with their craving for attention and their determination to turn every event into a benefit performance in their own favour, are lacking in genuine or sincere emotions. As far as Osborne's treatment of the type is concerned, the opposite is true. His characters may pass from one emotion to another with startling rapidity; the opinions they express may add up to a mass of inconsistencies and contradictions; their attitude to the characters around them may shift and veer; but beneath the turbulent surface there is always a core of genuine, heartfelt passion. In an often quoted comment made early in his career, Osborne declared that his object was to give his audiences 'lessons in feeling'[5]; and (although 'lesson' is an unduly didactic word which he might later have repudiated) the expression of feeling is always central to Osborne's successful plays. What constitutes that 'feeling' differs from play to play, for although Osborne's principal characters conform to a general type they are nevertheless an astonishingly diverse crew; but some kind of distress is always there, a helpless fury against the insufficiencies of the everyday world.

More than one critic has pointed out that Osborne's characters mostly experience emotions felt in *isolation*[6]. Their egocentricity cuts them off from others at the same time as they suffer an unbearable longing for some form of human or spiritual contact. This is a generalization, of course, and like all such should be treated with caution: certainly in his later plays Osborne's characters display a wary relaxation of tension and some genuine emotional contact with their companions. But it remains true that when we think of an Osborne play we usually think of one character, crystallized in one actor's performance; and that character's emotions are expressed not so much through the situation he finds himself in, with all the human relationships it involves, as in a constant flow of talk which is in some sense a rejection of that situation. Rather than live within it, he prefers to talk his way out of it. Not surprisingly, the drink flows freely in many of Osborne's plays, loosening tongues and breaking down the barriers of moderation which occasionally restrain even the actor type.

Thus a common criticism of Osborne is that his plays are one-man diatribes without the infrastructure of plot and the intricacies of character relationship required to make them fully dramatic. But despite the overbearing nature of his stormy protagonists, they do not exist in a total vacuum: the 'lesson in feeling' which Osborne conveys through their impassioned natures is tempered and sharpened by the delineation of the characters around them. Certain characteristic Osborne supporting roles recur, and although they may not be given much to say, they are drawn with sympathy and perception. Most important among them are the silent or downtrodden sufferers for whom the violent outbursts of the hero are not simply an exhilarating display of histrionics, but a direct and wounding attack—an indication of the painful clash of temperaments which almost inevitably accompanies any close relationship with the sort of individual I have characterized as the 'actor type'. The example *par excellence* is Alison, Jimmy Porter's browbeaten wife; the type includes Phoebe Rice in *The Entertainer* and, in more subtle form, Pamela's companion Constance in *Time Present*. Occasionally such characters play an important part in the drama although they are never seen: Bill Maitland's wife in *Inadmissible Evidence* is one such. In one of Osborne's most interesting plays, *A Patriot for Me*, Redl might be said to develop from the second sort of character to the first, the discovery of his homosexual nature being the turning-point which converts him from a passive, withdrawn figure into an expressive, temperamental individual with many of the distinctive marks of the actor type.

By contrast with these mutely suffering characters, who serve to expose the weakest and cruellest side of the hero's identity, there stand the easy-going sympathizers who manage to co-exist harmoniously with their more dominant companions, turning aside the stream of insults that comes their way with a good-natured shrug. Again the prime example comes from *Look Back in Anger*, where the imperturbable sympathy of Cliff Lewis acts as a perfect foil to Jimmy Porter's querulous outbursts. Although he is less important to the overall scheme of the play, Frank Rice occupies much the same role in relation to his father in *The Entertainer*; in *Luther* there is Martin's sympathetic superior Staupitz; in *Inadmissible Evidence* there is Maitland's chief clerk Hudson (until, by the end of the play, even his loyalty has been strained to breaking-point).

Osborne rings the changes on these relationships, and the minor characters are as varied, in their camouflaged way, as the heroes with whom they are in contact. As Osborne's work progresses the types tend to lose their distinctive edge; *The Hotel in Amsterdam* marks a point at which Osborne makes what Simon Trussler calls his 'most successful attempt to render with a degree of emotional realism a balanced group of characters rather than a hero around whom action and actors gravitate'[7]. This balance is maintained in *West of Suez*, but both plays still have one dominant figure—Laurie in *The Hotel in Amsterdam* and Wyatt Gillman in *West of Suez*; and significantly, as I shall suggest later, these two are both writers.

Although their nature forces them to the centre of attention, the relationship of Osborne's major characters with those around them is not ignored and indeed often forms a vital part of their painful emotional make-up. We have noted two characteristic supporting roles; before we leave the subject another interesting feature of the typical Osborne hero should be mentioned. It demonstrates itself in a variety of ways—sometimes in the characters present on stage, sometimes in the theme of the play, and sometimes in references that surface more or less randomly during one of the hero's monologues. With very few exceptions, the most intense of all the family relationships for an Osborne character is the parental bond, and the 'lessons in feeling' in his drama almost invariably touch on this subject in their most emotional moments.

Sometimes we see the hero in the role of parent, sometimes in that of the child; in particular it is the relationship between father and son or daughter that touches an Osborne protagonist to the quick. Once again, *Look Back in Anger* provides the model illustration: Jimmy Porter's most important speech is the one in which he reveals the primal source of his anger. 'For twelve months', he declares, 'I watched my father dying—when I was ten years old':

> All that that feverish failure of a man had to listen to him was a small, frightened boy. I spent hour upon hour in that tiny bedroom. He would talk to me for hours, pouring out all that was left of his life to one lonely, bewildered little boy, who could barely understand half of what he said. All he could feel was the despair and the bitterness, the sweet, sickly smell of a dying man ... You see, I learnt at an early age what it was to be angry—angry and helpless. And I can never forget it ... I knew more about love ... betrayal ... and death, when I was ten years old than you will probably ever know all your life. (p. 58)

In *The Entertainer* Archie Rice is seen both as father and as son. Act I ends with him breaking off in the middle of one his comic stories, turning to his daughter and appealing 'Talk to me'; the second act is built about his responsibility for the death of his own father after he has persuaded the old performer to return to the stage to save his failing road-show. Martin's inadequate relationship with his father is a major feature of *Luther*; in *Inadmissible Evidence* Bill Maitland's agonized apologia is delivered to his silent teenage daughter; in *Time Present* the shadow of Pamela's dying father lies across scene after scene; and the patriarchal figure of Wyatt Gillman dominates the family group in *West of Suez*.

Even the most generous admirer of Osborne is forced to admit that his towering character studies are not always reconciled with the strictest requirements of dramaturgy. In the preceding chapter it was argued that plot and character cannot be treated in isolation, since one depends so much upon the other; but there is no denying that in the indeterminate area of the playwright's craft where dramatic structure and psychological insight are welded together, it is the construction rather than the characterization which tends to let Osborne down. In his careful study of the dramatist, Simon Trussler has shown that Osborne is at heart a conventional dramatist and not infrequently a rather careless one[8]. He often, for instance, starts off with an exposition scene of unnecessary length, only to allow important developments to take place later off-stage. Sometimes, after a leisurely opening act, later scenes are crammed with action, some of it too hurried and episodic to make its full impact. There is, in fact, hardly a single play of Osborne's that is not a little weak at the seams.

As has already been suggested in our study of *Inadmissible Evidence*, and as I hope to show later in this chapter, Osborne substitutes a kind of linguistic structure for the more conventional structure of incident and plot, and it is this structure of language, robust and expressive but deftly and sometimes delicately orchestrated, which gives the best of his plays the sense of pace and progression they undeniably possess.

The hallmark of success in an Osborne play has always been the unfolding portraiture of a character in all its immediacy and particularity; and the medium of this portrayal has always been language rather than incident. But in the early stages of his career this was not the primary virtue that critics attributed to him. _Look Back in Anger_ proved a powerful weapon in the struggle to free the theatre from the tired and stultifying tradition of English drawing-room comedy. A move away from that tradition was, almost inevitably, a move to the left politically: the mid-1950s was a period when 'commitment' in the arts was discussed more anxiously than at any time since the embattled 1930s, and it was natural that Jimmy Porter's outbursts should seem to be the creation of a left-wing dramatist attuned to the particular frustrations of the 1950s. There are signs that Osborne, for a time, saw himself as first and foremost a Socialist dramatist harnessing his art to the cause of creating a better society[9]. Archie Rice, like Jimmy Porter although rather more oddly in view of his overall temperament, describes with evident relish and approval an old acquaintance for whom

> ... the most deadly four-letter word in the English—or any other—language, was Tory. He'd apply it to anything, provided he thought it was really bad enough.   (p. 64)

But it was not long before critics began pointing out that Jimmy Porter's antagonism towards the high Tory parents of his wife did not have much to do with any coherent form of Socialist conviction[10]; and, as we have already seen, the political aspects of _The Entertainer_ are lost sight of in the hurried action of the play's second half. It began to look as if Osborne, rather like Archie's friend, simply used 'Tory' as a term of abuse—a serious accusation to be levelled against a dramatist committed to an analysis of the failings of society, and one which the next stage of his career did nothing to remove.

After _Epitaph for George Dillon_, an early play written in collaboration with Anthony Creighton and revised for production after the success of _The Entertainer_, there came _The World of Paul Slickey_, Osborne's only musical and the most disastrous of the failures with which his career has been peppered. _Paul Slickey_ is partly a vicious attack on the ruthless and reckless frivolity of the gossip columnists of the English popular press (although Paul Slickey himself is portrayed with a curious blend of distaste and admiration), and partly a none-too-subtle satire upon the determination of the upper clases to sabotage the Welfare State by holding on to their wealth and position by every means within their power. Various other targets, most notably the contemporary church, loom in and out of focus, and irrelevantly but characteristically, Osborne brings the musical to a conclusion with the appearance of a miracle drug that will affect instant sex-change for those who would like to be a

> Woman at the weekend and a man all the week
> Two days as Madame Pompadour and five as an Ancient Greek.   (pp. 79–80)

Not surprisingly the musical opened to a unanimously hostile press, and fostered in Osborne a hatred of theatrical journalism which made an attack upon critics an almost mandatory set-piece in his later plays. More important, its superficial analysis of contemporary society put paid to any claim that might still be made for Osborne as a political dramatist. Osborne himself, whether or not as a direct result of the reception of *The World of Paul Slickey*, withdrew into the comparative safety of historical material for the subject-matter of his next two plays. *A Subject of Scandal and Concern*, Osborne's first (and for ten years his only) play for television, is a fairly straightforward dramatization of a nineteenth century incident, the trial and imprisonment of George Holyoake, the last Englishman to be punished by the law for blasphemy. It is sober but somewhat uninspired, touching upon the isolation of the individual, a familiar Osborne theme, but without the idiosyncratic vigour that marks his writing at its best.

Nevertheless, *A Subject of Scandal and Concern* did something to salvage Osborne's reputation; his next stage play, *Luther*, returned him to his rightful position as a major contemporary dramatist. *Luther* has its blemishes. Its 'epic' structure is conceived along Brechtian lines, but Brecht's principal object of diverting attention from the psychology of the individual towards broader social and political issues is largely ignored or mishandled. Osborne, as is well known, was attracted to the figure of Luther after reading Erik H. Erikson's psychoanalytical study *Young Man Luther*,[11] and the play is strongly influenced by the view that Luther's career has its basis in personal neurosis. Martin's relationship with his father, and above all the psychosomatic state of his bowels, are presented by Osborne as issues at least as important as the religious and intellectual premises which led to his break with Rome. But the virtues of *Luther* far outweigh its faults and the portrait of the tormented priest obsessed with his sluggish bowels as he struggles with his faith, however ludicrous it may sound, is expressed by Osborne in memorably cloacal imagery. *Luther* (and to a lesser extent *A Subject of Scandal and Concern*) had the effect of freeing him from the somewhat mechanical social protest which was an element in *The Entertainer* and almost the whole of *The World of Paul Slickey*, so that when he returned to the contemporary English scene in *Inadmissible Evidence* he was able to create an authentic hero of modern times whose sensibilities were not shackled by the trappings of 'commitment'. In the eyes of some critics, this was a betrayal of the causes for which the early Osborne had fought; in fact, it heralded the emancipation of his distinctive gift for the exploration of feeling through language.

Significantly, in an article written in 1961[12], Osborne, commenting on the developments he would like to see in the theatre of the 1960s, said nothing about the artist's duty to society:

> But what I would like most of all—although of course it's not something you can legislate for—is to see artists in the theatre being allowed to *play* at their work. Everything has to be so serious and specific all the time . . . Artists should have the right to relax, to be frivolous, to indulge themselves in their work.

By the end of the decade Osborne had earned the right to indulge himself in this element of 'play'. Precisely how far he had moved from the Socialist stance attributed to him by so many critics can be seen from the two plays *Time Present* and *The Hotel in Amsterdam*, which appeared in 1968. Set in a West End flat belonging to an MP (admittedly a Labour one) and an expensive Dutch hotel, respectively, they occupied the very same 'bourgeois' territory that the left-wing dramatists of the 1950s had so decisively abandoned. Pamela, the out-of-work actress and the central character of *Time Present*, is unashamedly right-wing: 'Tories like me are not "some people"', she reminds her companion sharply[13]. And it is interesting to note the colour in which Laurie, in *The Hotel in Amsterdam*, paints his family background:

> Retired rotten, grafting publicans, shop assistants, ex-waitresses. They live on and on. Having hernias and arthritic hips and strokes. But they go on: writing poisonous letters to one another. Complaining and wheedling and paying off the same old scores with the same illiterate signs. 'Dear Laurie, thank you very kindly for the cheque. It was most welcome and I was able to get us one or two things we'd had to go without for quite some time, what with me having been off work all this time and the doctor sends me to the hospital twice a week. They tell me it's improving but I can't say I feel much improvement. How are you, old son? Old son?'
>
> (p. 126)

Compare this with Jimmy Porter's attack on his wife's relatives in *Look Back in Anger*:

> The Platitude from Outer Space—that's brother Nigel. He'll end up in the Cabinet one day, make no mistake. But somewhere at the back of that mind is the vague knowledge that he and his pals have been plundering and fooling everybody for generations. . . . And nothing is more vague about Nigel than his knowledge. His knowledge of life and ordinary human beings is so hazy, he really deserves some sort of decoration for it—a medal inscribed 'For Vaguery in the Field'.
>
> (p. 20)

And then there are 'Mummy and Daddy':

> And don't let the Marquess of Queensberry manner fool you. They'll kick you in the groin while you're handing your hat to the maid.
>
> (p. 21)

The frustrated outbursts of the angry young man boiling with resentment against an outmoded class system have been replaced by the bickering of prosperous, privileged individuals living in fastidious isolation from the masses. We must, as always, beware of reading autobiographical material into the utterances of a dramatist's characters, but there can be little doubt that, as Osborne himself has climbed up the social scale, his characters have travelled with him, reflecting his new circumstances and surroundings and to some extent his changed opinions. As the social conscience diminishes, so the sense of 'play', or of freedom to explore opinions, ideas and characters without any sense of duty or obligation other than to his own talents, has been enlarged.

Every dramatist of any importance, it might be argued, needs a scale of values as a perspective against which to present his characters, giving depth and significance to the portrayal of their emotions and personal crises. Osborne's retreat from the scale of values associated with the notion of commitment can be charted fairly easily: it is more difficult to decide whether anything has replaced it. Does Osborne himself accept the scale of values of the 'actor types' he puts on the stage, with all their self-aggrandizement and pettiness? Certainly he invests a great deal of sympathy in his protagonists; but there is something else, far less tangible or easy to define, which runs through the majority of the plays and gives them an eccentric but identifiable foundation in a personal scheme of moral evaluation. That is what, for want of a better word, might be called Osborne's sense of patriotism.

'Patriotism, like honour, is one's own business', declares Jocelyn Broome in *The Gift of Friendship*[14]; and Osborne's patriotism is a deeply personal thing owing little to the conventional notions of service or public pride. Osborne's England is a landscape of the imagination rather than of historical reality. It is a strange world, more of a club than a country, whose members have passed certain strict tests. The capacity for suffering is one, the ability to articulate one's feelings is another. Tolerance of the deficiencies of others is not one of the qualifications: one consistent feature in Osborne's English plays is the view that contemporary society is suffering from a degeneration of feeling and language, and the hero's isolation becomes increasingly an impatient and wholesale rejection of modern times. In *Look Back in Anger* there is Jimmy Porter's famous complaint:

> There aren't any good, brave causes left. If the big bang does come, and we all get killed off, it won't be in aid of the old-fashioned, grand design. It'll just be for the Brave New-nothing-very-much-thank-you. (pp. 84–85)

As time goes on the young, the fashionable folk-heroes of the 1960s, are increasingly seen as major contributors to this degeneration. Bill Maitland's condemnation of his daughter, 'stuffed full of paltry relief for emergent countries, and marches and boycotts and rallies', has already been quoted; Pamela in *Time Present* is forever railing against the younger generation; and this particular strand of thought reaches a high point in *West of Suez*, in the contrast between Wyatt Gillman, with his nostalgic affection for 'something like a certain form of, say, cloud formation, called the English imagination'[15], and Jed, the rootless young American (and Americans, for Osborne, are almost as bad as the young) whose incoherent abuse of language and emotion stands for everything that Osborne detests.

Not surprisingly, the England that is summoned up in speech after speech from Osborne's characters turns back to the past. Jimmy Porter looks back in anger on his personal predicament, but he has a certain nostalgia for the old certainties of Britain's imperial grandeur:

> The old Edwardian brigade do make their brief little world look pretty tempting. All home-made cakes and croquet, bright ideas, bright uniforms. Always the same picture: high summer, the long days in the sun, slim volumes of verse, crisp linen, the smell of starch. What a romantic picture. Phoney too, of course. It must have rained sometimes. (p. 17)

And Alison's father, when he arrives to take her home, is a sympathetic figure, as ill at ease in contemporary society as Jimmy himself.

Rather similarly, Billy Rice's turn-of-the-century memories in *The Entertainer* point to a sharp contrast with his son's disreputable roadshow:

> We all had our own style, our own songs—and we were all English. What's more, we spoke English. It was different. We all knew what the rules were. We knew what the rules were, and even if we spent half our time making people laugh at 'em we never seriously suggested that anyone should break them. (p. 81)

In *West of Suez* the glimpse of a vanished past merges with the theme of parental relationships as Wyatt Gillman and his daughters recall their life in a nomadic colonial family:

EVANGIE: Do you remember Grandfather's study?
WYATT: What? The old boy's?
FREDERICA: I'll say.
WYATT: All my life . . .
EVANGIE: The joss sticks and Burmese guns. Saddle oil . . .
FREDERICA: Even the books smelt of curry powder. The Casino Palace, Port Said.
EVANGIE: Back numbers of *The Times of Natal*. A Zulu grammar.
FREDERICA: Manuals in Urdu.
EVANGIE: Rawhide shields and dried python skins and brass iguanas. And the photographs.
FREDERICA: Brown. Brown to yellow.
WYATT: The Casino Palace!
EVANGIE: The Groups.
WYATT: What did the old boy say? I know—'The Royal Navy always travels first class'. (p. 60)

In *A Sense of Detachment* the clash of past and present is presented in linguistic terms when extracts from a pornographer's catalogue, with its blunt four-letter monotony, alternate with the delicate emotional precision of passages of English verse.

Mention of *A Sense of Detachment*, that puzzling and disquieting anti-play in which a group of actors supposedly gathered together for a rehearsal, ruminate, improvise, recite snatches of poetry and song, and exchange insults with characters 'planted' among the audience, reminds us that any generalization about Osborne needs to be modified to take account of the extraordinary diversity of his dramatic output. His career has been marked by ceaseless experiments and new departures—many of them, it must be confessed, illuminated only by occasional flames from the authentic Osborne volcano.

Some of his minor works are adaptations from other authors. *A Bond Honoured*, Osborne's only brush with the National Theatre, was adapted from a play by Lope de Vega on the suggestion of Kenneth Tynan, who had left his reviewing to become the National's 'literary manager'. The enterprise came at a moment when interest in Antonin Artaud's Theatre of Cruelty was gathering momentum, and the adaptation's sensational theme (a sinner who commits every crime imaginable before retribution finally catches up with him) is matched by a rather aimless sensationalism in the dialogue and action, and is perhaps best forgotten as a misconceived venture from beginning to end. More recently Osborne has published two further adaptations. *The Picture of Dorian Gray*, styled 'A Moral Entertainment', adds little, if anything, by way of a fresh perspective on Wilde's novel, and failed to excite the critics when it reached the stage in 1975. More ambitiously, *A Place Calling Itself Rome* turns out to be an up-dated version of Shakespeare's *Coriolanus*. Of all Shakespeare's characters the most obvious candidate for comparison with a typical Osborne hero is the overbearing Roman who gives his name to this play. His disdain for the common masses, his ambiguous regard for his own country, and his eventual humiliation in a harrowing scene with his own mother, all offer parallels to themes which have preoccupied Osborne. Unfortunately Osborne confines himself to transferring the action to a hazily-defined modern setting and watering down Shakespeare's poetry to a limp contemporary equivalent. In place of Coriolanus' reply to his mother's appeal:

> O, mother, mother,
> What have you done? Behold! the heavens do ope,
> The gods look down, and this unnatural scene
> They laugh at. O my mother! mother! O!
> You have won a happy victory to Rome;
> But, for your son, believe it, O! believe it,
> Most dangerously you have with him prevailed,
> If not most mortal to him. But let it come. (V. ii, 182–9)

Osborne substitutes:

> Oh, Mother, Mother! What have you done? Look, everyone watches this scene and laughs at every single element in it. Oh Mother, Mother! Oh! You've won a skilful victory for Rome, but, for your son, believe it, Oh, believe it!—you don't know what you've done to *him*. But perhaps you do, and you were right to have done it. So be it ... (p. 74)

In the difficult work of adaptation, Osborne's hand seems to falter, and he rarely gives the impression that he is using another writer's insight as a starting-point for his own creativity—he appears rather to seize on certain obvious parallels with his own artistic interests and to exploit them with little of his customary linguistic subtlety.

There are other plays, particularly among those he has written for television, which barely belong to any category at all. *The Right Prospectus*, with which Osborne returned to the television screen ten years after *A Subject of Scandal and Concern*, is a not unsuccessful fantasy. A 'young-to-middle-aged' couple enrol as pupils in a public school: she makes a success of mixing with the youngsters, while he remains miserable and ineffectual. From time to time it highlights Osborne's bitter-sweet attitude towards the traditional privileges of the middle classes, particularly in the jocularly sadistic pep-talk delivered to the new arrival by the head of his house, a juvenile Osborne hero whose language is in the author's best tradition:

> You're neither in a doss house for scruffy-minded *New Statesman* wet eggs or the offspring of fecund women graduates and breast fed

from Aldermaston to Grosvenor bloody Square. You will come to me here—or wherever-I-happen-to-be—and you'll find me—every morning after Chapel until I tell you not to—and report. It's a daft system, the whole thing but so is the Divine bloody Office, *and* the democratic process, one man one vote, the technological revolution where even the tin-openers don't work let alone the money system and workers and industry and the thoughts of Chairman bloody Mao.

(p. 25)

Two more recent plays, *Very Like A Whale* and *The Gift of Friendship*, deal somewhat sombrely with the theme of encroaching old age, with its disillusionment and boredom—the first as it affects an industrial tycoon, knighted for his achievements as an exporter but unable to find satisfaction at home or at work, and the second as it creeps up on a writer immured in the study of his country house. They have their links with the main body of Osborne's work—*Very Like A Whale* in its impatience with the glibly patriotic self-justification of the industrial world, its anti-Americanism and its sense that the best of England's life is over ('London doesn't seem to belong to us any more', says the hero sadly, gazing at the tourists outside Buckingham Palace)[16], *The Gift of Friendship* in its preoccupation with the question of language and style as a mark of English civilization. But in both plays it is the themes rather than their treatment which remind us that Osborne is the author.

Osborne's ventures into the field of satire should perhaps concern us more closely, for here the link between the nature of the genre and Osborne's view of his native land is inevitably a close one. His unhappy satirical musical, *The World of Paul Slickey*, has already been mentioned. Two short plays, *The Blood of the Bambergs* and *Under Plain Cover*, which appeared in a double bill under the title *Plays for England* in 1962, might best be described as satires, and so too might *A Sense of Detachment*. Proportionally, satirical drama may not figure very largely in Osborne's output, but the mordant humour of the satirist is never far from the heart of his writing. It may seem odd, then, that his occasional attempts at pure satire have met with such little success. The two 'Plays for England' do not fall into quite the same dismal category of failure as *The World of Paul Slickey*; but, sandwiched between *Luther* and *Inadmissible Evidence*, they represent a noticeable dip in the author's development.

The Blood of the Bambergs was inspired by the excitement surrounding the nuptials of Princess Margaret and Tony Armstrong-Jones: it begins well with a splendid parody of the late Richard Dimbleby's awe-inspiring television commentaries on such occasions, but falters in an interview with one of the foremen overseeing the preparations:

> I myself, just in my section mind you, I have calculated that during the past seventeen years in which I have had the honour to do this job, I could have built, using the same materials and labour, you understand, twenty-seven secondary modern schools and one million two hundred thousand houses.
>
> (p. 20)

Osborne makes his point—that sham and outdated pageantry is diverting the country's resources away from its most pressing problems—but at the expense of abandoning subtlety in favour of overstatement, with the inevitable consequence that his wit becomes blunted. True to the tendency we have already mentioned, Osborne introduces a plethora of incident into the plot: the true bridegroom is killed in a motor accident, and in a desperate bid to keep things going a press photographer is made to stand in for him. He turns out to be an illegitimate step-brother of the ill-fated Prince Wilhelm, and the royal bride, for good measure, reveals that she is frigid. After various farcical adventures, the play rallies briefly with the reappearance of Wimple, 'scarcely breathing', to describe the ceremony for the nation's viewers:

> Now—as the royal couple, still kneeling on their faldstools, bow their heads before the Archbishop, the choir and congregation sing the cheerful and intensely singable hymn, personally chosen by the couple themselves, 'O Perfect Love'. In just a moment, with the final triumphant fanfare, sounded by trumpeters from the Prince's own regiment, the Royal Bamberger Blues, you will see the Prince and his bride slowly move along the aisle to the Great West Door. My goodness, what a uniquely impressive sight it all is! (p. 72)

Under Plain Cover suffers from the same multiplication of themes as *The Blood of the Bambergs*, only rather more disastrously. It begins with the portrayal of a couple whose marital harmony derives from their mutual liking for dressing up to indulge their sexual fantasies. For its time this was a daring theme, and Osborne contributed his mite to the liberation of the English stage by refusing to adopt an attitude of moral censure in the depiction of his couple poring over their clothing catalogues or growing nostalgic about the decline of the Directoire style of knickers. But this successful if scarcely epoch-making strand of the plot gets lost in a welter of misdirected fury when Osborne returns to the attack upon one of his favourite targets, popular journalism. The couple, it is discovered, are actually brother and sister, and the sensational exploitation by the press of their unwittingly incestuous marriage brings the play to an unsatisfactory conclusion, leaving the spectator in doubt as to whether the play is a plea for greater sexual freedom, a defence of the individual's right to privacy, or a more general commentary upon the hypocrisy of the English in and out of bed.

In *A Sense of Detachment*, too, the targets are diverse and unrelated. Experimental drama is pilloried in the self-mocking form of the play itself; the attitudes of the general public get no more sympathy in the vulgar interpolations from the pseudo-spectators planted in the auditorium, and the photographs and film sequences projected on to a screen, together with the random utterances of the actors, cover a variety of contemporary ills. But by far the larger part of the play is concerned with language: Osborne's shock tactics in forcing the audience to listen to the gross obscenities of the pornographic trade issuing from the prim mouth of a grey-haired actress have their desired effect, but the sequence is continued long after the point has been made. Here as elsewhere, Osborne seems to have been deflected from the course of artistic duty by his interest in the detailed particulars of sexual misbehaviour.

One reason, then, for Osborne's weakness as a satirist is his inability to focus his fire upon one target at a time; and another more intangible and more general failure in his writing contributes to this. He finds great difficulty in looking at something (or someone) he dislikes *objectively*

33

enough to make his treatment of the subject convincing. When his dialogue does not have a subjective origin linked to the mental processes of a character for whom he feels sympathy, he often turns to tired and disappointing phraseology. We have already seen one instance of this in the contrast between Maitland's credo in the opening dream sequence of *Inadmissible Evidence* and the savage brilliance of the rest of his dialogue; here are a couple of extracts from the opening scene of *Time Present*, where Pamela is haranguing her teenage step-sister:

> PAMELA: I suppose that hippie outside belongs to you?
> EDITH: Who?
> PAMELA: Does he have a name or is he a group? It was a bit difficult to tell if he was one or several. (p. 22)

> PAMELA: He's on what your children call a trip, Mama. Having un-memorable visions in a psychedelic, sort of holiday camp shirt and a racoon coat in my doorway. Trip clothes, right, Pauline?
> PAULINE: You just hate any sort of fun or anything. (p. 23)

Pamela, unpleasant though she may be, is credible down to the last syllable, and through her scornful description a far better picture is built up of the absent Dave than Osborne manages to create of Pauline despite her presence on the stage. Osborne's weakness is the reverse side of his strength. When he centres his picture of England upon a character with whom he feels creative sympathy, it springs to immediate life; when he tackles a subject directly without the mediation of such a character all too often it becomes flat, trivial and without interest.

Some of the features that go together to make an Osborne play have been described in the preceding pages: the chapter would be incomplete without a more detailed examination of one or two individual plays. Osborne himself is resolutely opposed to critics: they 'should be regularly exposed', he once wrote, 'like corrupt constabularies or faulty sewage systems'. 'Theatrical ideas', he insists, 'are theatrically expressed and not in the literal-minded manner of literary weeklies. ... They are organic, and when they work they can be seen to be working'[17]. Inevitably one sets about dissecting Osborne's drama with a certain feeling of diffidence; and, as I have suggested, the true quality of his plays is sometimes impervious to formal criticism. But, for better or for worse, I have chosen to compare his three earliest plays with two of his most recent ones in the attempt to provide a few modest pointers to his progress and development.

Of Osborne's first three plays (after his earlier, unpublished and unpublicized works), the latest to appear on the London stage was actually written before *Look Back in Anger* and *The Entertainer*. How far the final version of *Epitaph for George Dillon* differs from the original, and how much of a hand Osborne's collaborator Anthony Creighton had in the work, has not been revealed; but it seems reasonable to take George Dillon, the frustrated and none too scrupulous actor-writer around whom the action revolves, as the first of Osborne's characteristic heroes. On the whole the play gives the impression of being badly tailored to suit Osborne's particular talents. It is set in a lower-middle class suburban household, gloomily observed in all its details and occasionally spilling over into caricature, with its anxious mum, silent dad and a trio of daughters—two of them unimaginatively accepting their surroundings, the third seething with suppressed indignation at the triviality of her life—coexisting dully in a house cluttered with tasteless furniture. George Dillon is pitched into this *ménage* when Mrs Elliott invites him to stay with them during one of his periods out of work, and the action which develops forms the material of a fairly conventional plot. Dillon seduces the youngest and most bovine of the Elliott daughters, but strikes up more of an intellectual rapport with Ruth, the eldest, whose long-running affair with a writer has just come to an unhappy end. Dillon is trapped into a marriage with the pregnant Josie, and sees his hopes of an escape from mediocrity evaporate when his first play, retitled 'Telephone Tart' and doctored beyond recognition by a seedy impresario, opens to 'capacity business' on its provincial tour, bolstering his finances but putting paid to his vaguely-defined ideals:

> Shall I recite my epitaph to you? Yes, do recite your epitaph to me. 'Here lies the body of George Dillon; aged thirty-four—or thereabouts—who thought, who hoped, he was that mysterious, ridiculous being called an artist. He never allowed himself one day of peace. He worshipped the physical things of this world, and was betrayed by his own body. He loved also the things of the mind, but his own brain was a cripple from the waist down. He made no one happy, no one look up with excitement when he entered the room . . .'
> (p. 87)

Occasionally a flash of Osborne rhetoric lights up the play—usually when Dillon is referring to his theatrical experience:

> Listen: all I ever got—inside and outside of the theatre—is the raves of a microscopic minority, and the open hostility of the rest. I attract hostility. I seem to be on heat for it. Whenever I step out on to those boards—immediately, from the very first moment I show my face—I know I've got to fight almost every one of those people in the auditorium. Right from the stalls to the gallery, to the Vestal Virgins in the boxes!
> (p. 56)

But even such passages as this lose much of their impact inside the plot which the authors have devised. It is difficult to imagine a figure like Dillon, however hard-up he might be, involving himself so deeply in a household as depressing as that of the Elliots. 'Put any one of them on a stage', as he declares himself:

> . . . and no one would take them seriously for one minute! They think in clichés, they talk in them, they even feel in them—and, brother, that's an achievement
> (p. 58)

The jibe is, alas, all too true; with the exception of Ruth the Elliots are observed superficially and externally and fall victim to Osborne's inability to deal convincingly with characters for whom he has no sympathy. Dillon's supposed likeness to Mrs Elliot's son who was killed in the war provides a convenient reason for introducing him into the household, but the theme is developed no further; another unresolved strand of the plot concerns the discovery, after he has put Josie 'in the family way', that

Dillon is already married. 'It's simply that _____ fe nor I have ever bothered about a divorce', explains _____ [18]; and all is forgiven when it is discovered that, under _____ his wife is the family favourite in a television parlour ga_____

For all its weaknesses, *Epitaph for George Dillon* has an identifiable theme, closely linked to the structure of the play. Dillon may be shiftless and unprincipled; for all the evidence that is presented to the audience, his talents as a dramatist may be entirely imaginary; but of the gradual extinction of his ambitions as the Elliot household envelops him and welcomes his spurious success there can be no doubt. The play presents a clash between the sensibilities of the artist and the mediocrity of contemporary English culture; but the authors have buried the theme under irrelevancies like Dillon's former marriage and obscured it with the introduction of unnecessary minor characters like Norah Elliot, a shadowy third sister, and Barney, a down-at-heel showman who turns out to be an admirer of Hitler. Most of Osborne's later plays have an untidy plot-structure, but in *Epitaph for George Dillon* this defect is more obtrusive because the play observes the conventions of the well-made naturalistic play more closely than anything that was to follow. As Simon Trussler puts it, the play is full of 'the very weaknesses of the drawing-room family dramas whose conventions Osborne tried and failed to adapt, but was very soon to transcend'[19]. Conceived as a cry of protest against the stifling commercialism of the English theatre, it fails because its authors have made concessions to the very ills it is objecting to.

Look Back in Anger marks a partial but significant step forward for Osborne; there is little attempt to disguise it as a conventional 'well-made' play, and Osborne's true gift of theatrical invective is poured into a much looser structure. The play suffers from time to time from a somewhat melodramatic overstatement (witness, for instance, Jimmy Porter's speech about the death of his father, already quoted). Osborne's talents flow most naturally in the passages where Jimmy Porter simply elaborates on one or other of his favourite themes:

> There is no limit to what the middle-aged mummy will do in the holy crusade against ruffians like me. Mummy and I took one quick look at each other, and, from then on, the age of chivalry was dead. I knew that, to protect her innocent young, she wouldn't hesitate to cheat, lie, bully and blackmail. Threatened with me, a young man without money, background or even looks, she'd bellow like a rhinoceros in labour—enough to make every male rhino for miles turn white, and pledge himself to celibacy. (p. 52)

At one level, then, *Look Back in Anger* is a freewheeling, self-indulgent portrait of a typical Osborne actor type whose abrasive personality, for all its querulous selfishness and indeed cruelty, commands our sympathy in its constant battle against everyday mediocrity. For many, including Osborne himself, Jimmy's bad-mannered rejection of middle-class *mores* was seen as the clarion call of a neglected generation; as we have already argued, time has shown that the element of social protest is not so important to the play as it seems. But, as Harold Hobson noted in his review of the Royal Court production, 'there are really two plays in *Look Back in Anger*'[20]. The first thrusts itself forward in every word that Jimmy Porter utters, while the second emerges from a study of the long-suffering Alison and her relationship with her husband. In terms of its structure, this 'second' play is straightforward, even simple. Jimmy Porter despises his wife for her incapacity to share his anguished emotions. Finally goaded into the only gesture of defiance she can muster, she returns to her parents, enabling Jimmy to have a brief affair with her friend Helena. Unknown to Jimmy, Alison is pregnant, and in the loss of her child she experiences the mixture of pain and humiliation that enables the two to come to terms.

If *Look Back in Anger* is 'two plays', Harold Hobson preferred the second, while Kenneth Tynan nailed his influential colours to the mast of the first. In his judicious account of the play, Simon Trussler returns, by and large, to the second, labelling it 'basically a well-made problem play of considerable psychological insight'[21].

There are of course occasions when two distinct levels in a play can make the whole work rich and complex, but *Look Back in Anger* is hardly one of them. Point by point, the details of Trussler's argument are convincing enough, but the psychological study of Jimmy and Alison is not what makes the play exceptional—many another competent dramatist could have done as well—while Jimmy Porter's dialogue is something that Osborne alone could have produced and which, in many of its essential features, is almost independent of his relationship with Alison. Furthermore, although Osborne has worked hard to give Jimmy's resentful character a grounding in personal experience—his own suffering while his father lay dying, and Alison's inability to share his emotions—little that Jimmy Porter says gives much of a clue to his day-to-day existence. His chosen occupation as a sweetstall marketeer is mentioned from time to time, but of the activities it involves his language shows no trace. At least George Dillon, 'on heat' for hostility, has a lively appreciation of what it is like to be an actor; it is difficult to imagine Jimmy talking in such animated terms about the customers at his sweetstall or—looking forward to the later Osborne—to build up such a vivid picture of his working life as Osborne gives us of Maitland in *Inadmissible Evidence*. Jimmy Porter's rhetoric, then, the most distinctive feature of the play, exists in a kind of vacuum, largely detached from his own experience both in his private life and at work. It is this, of course, which leads Michael Billington to declare that Jimmy's character is modelled on the raw experience of an actor's frustrating life.

In *The Entertainer* the central character is an actor through and through, and it is this which makes it the most successful of the three plays, although in comparison even with the deficiences of *Epitaph for George Dillon* and *Look Back in Anger* its plot is a very patchy affair. Too many themes are introduced without being fully explored, from Jean's differences with her boyfriend to Archie's devious manoeuvres to counteract bankruptcy; and in particular the political confusion in the year of the Suez campaign, upon which attention should have been concentrated by the death of Archie's son, gets a very superficial treatment.

For all its failings *The Entertainer* gets closer to the qualities which Osborne defines as 'theatrical ideas theatrically expressed'. His theatrical powers, as we have stressed, are mainly concentrated within language, and in the dialogue of Archie Rice, the music-hall comedian whose twice-nightly vulgarity is introduced into the structure of the play, Osborne for the first time created the coherent, idiosyncratic imagery which gives his best plays their unity.

The device of cutting from scenes in the Rice household to the stage of an imaginary music-hall where Archie is working through his patter is simple but effective. Some seventeen years later, after *Oh What A Lovely War!* and its numerous successors have accustomed theatregoers to the equation of popular entertainment with the state of the nation's soul, it is easy to forget what a startling effect Archie Rice's first entry before a drop-curtain must have had when Sir Laurence Olivier created the role in 1957. Now that the shock has worn off, it should be easier to measure the more lasting artistic achievement of the technique.

'The music hall is dying', wrote Osborne in a Note to the play,

> ... and, with it, a significant part of England. Some of the heart of England has gone; something that once belonged to everyone, for this was truly a folk art ... Not only has this technique its own traditions, its own convention and symbol, its own mystique, it cuts right across the restrictions of the so-called naturalistic stage. Its contact is immediate, vital, and direct.

The Note sets out Osborne's motives clearly enough. But it is important to realize that Archie's solo spots, while they may be an 'anti-naturalistic' method of linking the family fortunes to an impressionistic picture of a vanishing England, are also an extension of Archie's own character just as, in a very different key, Martin's sermons in *Luther* throw more light upon the personality of the priest than upon the details of his dispute with Rome.

As a comedian, Archie uses the technique of the 'running gag', the joke that is introduced and repeated, with variations, throughout the show, and within the structure of the play this barrage of wisecracks adds up to a lurid verbal portrait of Archie's private personality, enabling his disarrayed sensibilities to find their expression in appropriate imagery. The patter itself is often second-rate stuff, faithfully modelled upon the material with which the music-hall tried vainly to attract its patrons in the years of its decline; but this quality is deliberate, and filtered through the nervy exhibitionism of the entertainer's dialogue is the coarsened but defiant personality of the man himself. Every running joke in *The Entertainer* has its dark underside, progressively revealed as the play proceeds. The income-tax man, an easy target for the professional performer, becomes a shadowy symbol of the material insecurity that haunts Archie. It is introduced casually enough when Archie returns home to find his daughter Jean has arrived:

> I haven't got my glasses on. I thought you were the income-tax man sitting there. I thought we had shaken him off. (p. 34)

The last time he paid income tax was in 1936, he boasts; and then he was 'trapped in hospital with a double hernia ... when two men in bowlers and rain-coats sprang at me from behind the screens'[22]. When a policeman calls at the door to deliver the news that Mick has been killed, Archie's evasive response is predictable:

> It's the income-tax man. It's the income-tax man. Tell him I've been expecting him. I've been expecting him for twenty years.
> (p. 73)

Finally, in the knowledge that ruin awaits him, he goes on stage to confront his last audience, regretting only his failure to 'notch up twenty-one against the income-tax man':

> There's a bloke at the side here with a hook, you know that, don't you? He is, he's standing there. I can see him. Must be the income-tax man. (p. 87)

Archie's ailing finances give his life a permanent sense of crisis; his hectic existence, always teetering on the brink of dislocation, is governed by the irrational forces of sex and alcohol. Like many actor types, Archie is loquacious on the subject of his sexual drives. 'You wouldn't think I was sexy to look at me, would you!' he boasts to his audience, and the words turn from a casual joke into a confession of his shabby lechery[23]. 'Thank God I'm normal!'—Archie injects the phrase into his first song, and it becomes a kind of refrain, at one moment merging with a flippant, half-cynical and half sentimental patriotism:

> Thank God we're normal, normal, normal.
> Thank God we're normal.
> We are the country's flower,
> And when the great call comes,
> Someone will gaze down on us,
> And say: They made no fuss—
> For this was their finest shower. (p. 61)

While at another it leads into a drunken confession of his own sexuality:

> Say, aren't you glad you're normal? I've always been a seven day a week man myself, haven't I, Phoebe? A seven day a week man. I always needed a jump at the end of the day—and at the beginning too usually. Just like a piece of bacon on the slab. Well, it's everybody's problem. (p. 73)

As for alcohol, Archie's fondness for draught Bass is first mentioned in the middle of his anecdote about the double hernia and the income-tax collectors, and it becomes a symbol for the spark of personality that keeps Archie on the failing show-business circuit when he could take up a remunerative job offered him in Canada. 'Anyway you can't buy draught Bass in Toronto', he announces, and that clinches the argument[24]. In the next scene this identification, rather less effectively, becomes explicit during an argument between Jean and her father:

> Listen, kiddie, you're going to find out that in the end nobody really gives a damn about anything except some little animal something. And for me that little animal something is draught Bass. (p. 76)

These repetitive catchphrases become a natural metaphor for Archie's confusion of the realities of life with the seedy *bonhomie* he projects across the footlights. Archie is a man trapped behind his own comic mask, unable to analyse his financial affairs except in terms of mocking references to the income-tax man, treating the decay of his marriage as an extended blue joke, and laughing away the dissipation of his talents with boastful talk of his consumption of draught Bass. The formal plot which, as we have seen, leaves much to be desired is less important than the development of mood and tempo carried forward in Archie's dialogue. Simon Trussler observes of Archie's solo spots that they 'fail to *connect* with the family episodes'[25]; this is certainly true at the simple level of plot-structure, but there is a kind of progressive linkage between the jokes that he hurls at his audience and the evasive raillery with which he batters his own family. The sharp contrast between the naturalistic family portrait of the opening scene and Archie's first 'spot' is clearcut and deliberate, but in the course of the play the alternating scenes complement each other in building up a composite picture of Archie's personality at its moment of crisis.

More to the point is Trussler's complaint that they 'never relate his own failure to the national decadence they parody and proclaim'[26]. Osborne's Note to the play (already quoted) confirms that *The Entertainer* was not written simply to illustrate the psychology of an interesting individual: from time to time oblique parallels are declared between his own shiftless morality and the general delapidation of the country. Archie's road show, with its nude Britannia and its tawdry appeal to patriotic sentiment, reflects Britain's tarnished grandeur after the Suez *débâcle* as clearly as Billy Rice's nostalgic memories of the music hall in its heyday recall the certainties of an imperial past.

But what of Archie himself? His first song has the refrain 'Why should I bother to care?' (taken up, with heavy sentimentality, in the closing scene); and Archie's refusal—or inability—to 'care' is a signal feature of his character. It is all too evident in the treatment of his own family, and is obviously related to his speech in praise of that 'little animal something' which he finds in draught Bass. But from time to time this refusal to allow any sort of moral feeling to interrupt the course of natural selfishness is seen as a national characteristic. 'We're all out for good old number one', he sings in his second appearance before the spotlights, and continues, as a Union Jack descends from the flies:

> Those bits of red still on the map
> We won't give up without a scrap.
> What we've got left back
> We'll keep—and blow you, Jack!
> Oh, number one's the only one for me!   (p. 33)

The identification of Archie's character with the moral decay of the nation is made most memorably in one of Osborne's characteristic confrontations between father and daughter:

> You see this face, you see this face, this face can split open with warmth and humanity. It can sing, and tell the worst, unfunniest stories in the world to a great mob of dead, drab erks and it doesn't matter, it doesn't matter. It doesn't matter because—look at my eyes. I'm dead behind these eyes. I'm dead, just like the whole inert, shoddy lot out there. It doesn't matter because I don't feel a thing, and neither do they. We're just as dead as each other.   (p. 72)

The revelation of 'old Archie, dead behind the eyes', has become almost as famous as Jimmy Porter's lament for the loss of 'good, brave causes'; and like the earlier speech of Archie's, although it is partially a tract for the times, it is summoned up by deep personal emotions. The entertainer is preparing his daughter for the news that he intends to leave Phoebe and marry again; and it comes just before the climax of the second act, when Mick's death is announced to the family. There is something unconvincing about Archie's plan to abandon Phoebe: one feels that it is introduced to demonstrate the extreme to which his moral emptiness has carried him, not that it arises naturally out of his character. And similarly his sense of identification with 'the whole inert, shoddy lot out there', while momentarily impressive, does not add up to a coherent statement about contemporary society, organically linked to the rest of the play.

Osborne has clearly attempted to expand the notion of an unfeeling society 'dead behind the eyes' in his treatment of the characters of Archie's two children Jean and Frank. Both are idealists whose illusions crumble as the play progresses. Frank is the conscientious objector whose altruistic pacifism does not stand up to the test of his brother's death: 'Those bloody wogs', he cries: 'They've murdered him'[27].

Jean, who begins as a left-wing intellectual attending rallies in Trafalgar Square and 'teaching Art to a bunch of Youth Club kids'[28], ends on a note of near-despair:

> Here we are, we're alone in the universe, there's no God, it just seems that it all began by something as simple as sunlight striking on a piece of rock. And here we are. We've only got ourselves. Somehow, we've just got to make a go of it. *We've only ourselves.* (p. 85)

But Frank's sudden conversion is crude and unsubtle, and Jean's rhetoric is strained and artificial. The grand design of *The Entertainer* is ambitious and rather muddled; but when the theme coincides with Archie Rice's dialogue what might be major defects in another author's play become simply minor irritations in a play whose language touches upon the nerve of psychological truth and, occasionally, opens up a rich and ambiguous perspective on the author's native land.

It is instructive to turn from *The Entertainer* to two of Osborne's most recent plays. The changes are considerable, and the most striking feature is perhaps the disappearance of the grand thematic statements about contemporary society which were built in to the earlier play without being fully worked out. Instead, we find that Osborne has diverted his attention to a careful and skilful modulation of the pace and temper of his drama. The credibility of the minor characters is improved, and their relationship with the central protagonist is more relaxed. Gone are the exaggerated theatrical climaxes which punctuated the earlier play; in their place Osborne has succeeded, through the accuracy and inventiveness of his dialogue, in creating and sustaining a particular mood, an atmosphere that is a combination of time, place and personality. Instead of the energetic but vague lambasting of Britain that we find in *The Entertainer*, there is a narrower but more exact picture of an England defined through the sensibilities of a group of individuals.

Earlier in this chapter I suggested that the England of Osborne's plays has something exclusive about it. Certainly it never approaches Shakespearian amplitude; all the same it expands and contracts its boundaries from one play to another. There are times when the little world of his characters, with their private jokes, thoughtless contempt for practically everyone who does not belong to their own tight circle, and equally groundless conviction of their own superiority, calls to mind nothing so much as the conversation of a company of actors as they unburden themselves after a performance. There are times, however, when it transcends the limitations of green-room gossip to become a vision, obliquely glimpsed, of a civilization and its discontents. The two extremes are well represented by *The Hotel in Amsterdam* and *West of Suez*.

The Hotel in Amsterdam is an attractive if rather slight play. It has no discernible theme and, until the dramatic news of a suicide in its closing minutes, virtually no action. It is a study of six friends whose characters are revealed in relaxed conversation as they lounge in an expensive Dutch hotel: here, if anywhere, Osborne allows himself the artist's right to indulge 'the element of *play*' in his work. The three couples have escaped by a variety of subterfuges from 'K.L.', the high-pressure film tycoon for whom four of them work. The prevailing mood is one of relief; 'For a few blessed days', says Laurie contentedly, 'No K.L. in our lives'[29].

Within the protection of their luxurious hideaway they abandon themselves to the trivia of life, wasting an inordinate amount of time in ordering drinks and planning expeditions, discussing their families, abusing K.L. and spinning out fantasies to keep the conversation going. Towards the end Laurie, the writer of the group, finds himself alone with Annie, and declares his love for his friend's wife[30]. But such is the bond of mutual affection holding the group together that even this revelation does nothing to disturb the balance. Occasionally the play edges towards a few comments on the stranglehold upon contemporary culture exercised by the likes of K.L. Here, for instance, is Laurie in a characteristic attack upon his hated employer:

> The world's full of hustlers and victims all beavering away to be pressed into K.L.'s service. Someone always wants to be useful or flattered or gulled or just plain whipped slowly to death or cast out into the knacker's yard by King Sham. Well, let him go ahead and get himself crucified this time. I know him not. (p. 94)

The agonies of his creative processes as a writer are inevitably tangled up with this theme:

> I work my drawers off and get written off twice a year as not fulfilling my early promise by some philistine squirt drumming up copy, someone who's got as much idea of the creative process as Dan's mother and mine rolled into one lazy minded lump of misery who ever battened off the honest efforts of others. (p. 99)

Laurie's dialogue invests him with a sharply-defined character whose language draws on the material of his own existence as vividly as Archie's in *The Entertainer*; but there is no attempt to diagnose the nation's soul through him as there was through Archie. Again, it is clear that the writer's travail and its shallow dismissal by the critics are subjects close to Osborne's heart, and it may well be that Laurie's opinions reflect those of his author; but it would surely be wrong to suggest that through them Osborne is making any general statement about the artist in society. Their tone is personal, and they become part of the tapestry of words that is *The Hotel in Amsterdam*, along with the other subjects—most of them traditionally taboo in polite society—that include pregnancy, menstruation, allusions to the horrors of the parental home, homosexuality, and some running jokes about air hostesses:

DAN: My mother would have made a good air hostess.

LAURIE: Your mother! Listen, my mother should have been Chief Stewardess on Monster's Airlines. She'd have kept you waiting in every bus, withheld information and liquor, snapped at you, and smirked at you meaninglessly or simply just ignored you.

DAN: Have you ever thought of airlines for homosexuals?

LAURIE: I say: what a splendid idea. You could call it El Fag Airlines.

ANNIE: Gus could be a stewardess.

LAURIE: We'd design him a divine outfit. I say I feel better already.   (p. 92)

Insubstantial but enjoyable, the conversation goes on, defining the characters rather than developing them, until Laurie's sister-in-law arrives, seeking companionship in the middle of some desperate crisis[31].

Gillian's arrival 'has broken the fragile spell', as the stage direction tells the reader, and on this occasion Osborne has succeeded in creating a convincing although unsympathetic character. Her nervous self-consciousness and eager, conventional gossip destroy the insubstantial world that Laurie and the others have built up for themselves:

GILLIAN: Tell me what else you've been doing. It does sound good. I've always wanted to come to Amsterdam . . . Did you go on the canal?

DAN: Yes.

GILLIAN: And that modern art gallery, whatever it's called. Can't pronounce Dutch. And the harbour, or where is it, where all the tarts sit in the windows looking like dolls. This hotel looks splendid . . . Do you think I can get a room? Perhaps I could get one down the hall. All I need is a little room.   (p. 131)

Shortly after Gillian's appearance news reaches the party that K.L. has locked himself in his study and committed suicide. The tyrant who dominated their lives could not, it seems, live without them. Osborne has once again fallen victim to his penchant for unnecessarily melodramatic endings. K.L.'s death and the idle conversation which has preceded it over two acts do little to illuminate one another, and this sudden intrusion of tragedy destroys the comic fabric which Osborne had sustained so successfully until the very last minutes of the play.

The pattern to which *West of Suez* is cut is very similar to that of *The Hotel in Amsterdam*. The mood again is one of escape and relaxation: instead of a weekend in Holland, Wyatt Gillman and his family are on a more extended stay with relatives on an unnamed tropical island, formerly an outpost of the British Empire. Once again there is nothing much to do except to drink and talk, and once again the relationships between the characters are marked by a sense of ease and fullness that was lacking in the earlier plays. A writer, too, is the central character of *West of Suez*; and, like *The Hotel in Amsterdam*, the play ends with an unexpected death.

43

Whereas one of the virtues of *The Hotel in Amsterdam* is that it is a play in which Osborne has freed himself from the urge to make violent but confused pronouncements about the state of his country, in *West of Suez* there is a recognizable concern for the quality of England, in particular the England that is shaped out of language; and despite a frail plot the carefully balanced structure of the play is largely directed towards this end. The 'tactful Hotel Empire' style of the suite in Amsterdam ('better than that rotten Paris', declares Laurie)[32], provides a deliberately characterless locale; but the setting for *West of Suez*, as the enigmatic title perhaps suggests, brings the action nearer home. Lamb, the expatriate writer, describes the island before independence:

> Before? Oh, not so very different I suppose. The Governor General's house is still there though he's called something else now; Royalty of some sort came out. New flag went up. The police band played the dreadful National Anthem, all deliciously out of tune; you couldn't believe it, the comedy and pain of it. I think someone actually recorded it as a collector's item. Some relief, I suppose. A bit of apprehension but not over much. The climate was the same, the people were the same, we were the same. Except . . . You see . . . There was despair in a lot of hearts. (p. 61)

The shadow of English imperial greatness in decline hangs over *West of Suez*, and merging with this melancholy theme is an ever-present sense of human mortality. Whereas the news of K.L.'s suicide simply terminates a mood in a rather arbitrary way, Wyatt's death, although equally unexpected, seems an integral part of *West of Suez*.

Asked to describe himself by his interviewer, Wyatt replies:

> I think I'm probably what my daughter Frederica says she is, just a lot of hot shit, if you'll pardon the expression, blood, vanity and a certain prowess. (p. 74)

Wyatt's son-in-law Edward is a pathologist—'just a plain old blood and shit man', he calls himself[33]. We see very little of him after the opening scene, but he strikes up a friendship with Jed, the young American, which worries his wife; and he reappears at the end of the play along with the rest to listen to Jed's outburst. The American student is, in his way, another blood and shit man:

> You know . . . what we think of you? Fuck all your *shit*—that's what we think. . . . The only thing that matters, man, is blood, man. Blood . . . You know what that means? No, no, you surely as to hell don't. No, no, when you pigs go, it ain't going to be no fucking fourth of July. All I see, and I laugh when I see it, man, I laugh, is you pigs barbecued, barbecued in your own shit. (pp. 82–83)

'Shit, blood, vanity and a certain prowess': this bleak combination of physical and mental attributes is the condition of man to which, as long as it lasts, the characters in *West of Suez* have to reconcile themselves. But predictably it does not generate much humility within the group. Like the characters in *The Hotel in Amsterdam*, they are a tightly-knit, exclusive set whose private jokes and shared memories serve to barricade them against the rest of the world. Whereas the group in the earlier play is drawn together by its antagonism to the overshadowing menace represented by K.L., here the bond that unites the characters is a more subtle one. It begins with the irrational ties that hold the family together (Wyatt himself and his sharp-tongued daughter Frederica have many of the waspish characteristics of the Osborne actor type, and their relationship perhaps forms the emotional core of the play); but other inhabitants of the island are drawn in, including Alastair, the queer Scots hairdresser, Harry, the 'hulking American' who escapes the general ban placed on Americans ('You're *special*', Wyatt tells him)[34], and Lamb, the wealthy, tax-avoiding novelist. Then there is Wyatt's secretary Christopher, a vaguely amiable background figure who makes an ineffectual confession of love to Frederica in the final scene. Naturally, other characters are excluded—American tourists, mothers-in-law and the disquieting Jed—while Mrs James, the island's star reporter whose icy inquisition of Wyatt is in some senses the climax of the play, remains a detached, impersonal figure.

All of the insiders have an emotional capacity that the others lack, from Alastair with his 'crying jags' to the apparently ineffectual Christopher, who reveals that during the war he killed an unarmed SS man, and then the GI who tried to stop him[35]. All of them would recognize Wyatt's analysis of his own feelings:

> Always weary, ineffably bored, always in some sort of vague pain and always with a bit of unsatisfying hatred burning away in the old inside like a heartburn or indigestion. (p. 70)

The 'unsatisfying hatred' smouldering within the aged Wyatt links him with the long line of Osborne heroes stretching back to Jimmy Porter and George Dillon. On its own it is a negative quality: Jed, too, has been generously endowed with the same passion. What translates Wyatt's personality into something more is the sense that Wyatt is one of the last representatives of a particular civilization, as undefinable as the 'certain form of, say, cloud formation, called the English imagination'[36], but unmistakable nevertheless.

Although his bumbling, self-deprecating affability and his outmoded slang conceal both malice and deliberate affectation, Wyatt Gillman is one of Osborne's most likeable protagonists. Like many of Osborne's characters he possesses not so much courage as audacity in expressing an unconventional morality. Talking about the First World War, he recalls

> being chased by a horde of women, very middle-class sort of women, half way across Southsea because I wasn't in uniform. Jolly thankful I was too. Too feeble to be conchie and too much of a funk to face all that mud and bullying and limbs blown off. (p. 41)

His patriotism, then, is not to be identified with physical bravado: it is almost exclusively concerned with feelings, memories, subtle gradations of the emotions: and this inevitably brings Wyatt face to face with the question of language. The sleepless Frederica's detestation of birds (one of the running themes of the play) leads Wyatt into a characteristically mock-modest declaration:

> Frederica is right as usual. Birds chatter and *that* is their mortal flaw. Chatter sins against language and when we sin against the word, we sin against God. Gosh, I *am* pompous. (p. 57)

The theme, presenting language and national identity as different sides of the same thing, surfaces emphatically in Wyatt's interview with Mrs James. Talking about religion he praises

> ... the King James Bible and the English genius to boot, which is being booted very swiftly, oh and good old Cranmer's Book of Common Prayer. It's like the Bible, it combines profundity without complexity. (p. 73)

'I still cling pathetically to the old bardic belief that "words alone are certain good"', he tells her a few moments later[37].

Implicit throughout the play is the suggestion that Wyatt—or the society in which he finds himself—is not entirely guiltless of the destruction of this linguistic heritage. After all, *he* chatters a lot, and near the beginning of the play Edward protests that such a distinguished figure as Wyatt

> ... shouldn't have to clown about doing interviews and literary quiz games and being a fireside character or sage or whatever he is to people ... (p. 22)

Nevertheless, it is left to Jed's mindless nihilism to deliver the final blow to the fabric of language so precious to Wyatt:

> Do you understand one word, those old words you love so much, what I mean? No. And you won't. If it ain't written down, you don't believe it ... There's only word left and you know what that is. It's fuck, man. Fuck ... That's the last of the English for you babies. Or maybe shit. (p. 83)

Once again, dealing with a character to whom he has no liking, Osborne overstates the case; and the cascade of obscenities with which Jed showers the assembled company has a magnificent shock effect in the theatre, but lacks the powerful psychological sympathy which gives such detailed credibility to the rest of the characters in *West of Suez*. Osborne comes close to destroying his case by stating it too bluntly.

After Jed's outburst it only remains for Wyatt to meet his end, shot down by armed islanders who appear out of the darkness. He is killed, presumably, as a result of the gratuitously insulting remarks about the island he had made in his interview for the local paper—although Osborne carefully leaves the assassins' motives unexplained. In the final epigram—'My God—they've shot the fox ...'—Osborne reveals once again his weakness for strong endings apparently crammed with significance but in fact somewhat tenuously linked to what has gone before. It doubtless makes the point that figures like Wyatt Gillman, with their paternalistic condescension towards those who do not belong to their own closed circle, represent a civilization which for all its faults at least spurs its opponents into creative opposition. Jed in one way, and the militant islanders in another, have rejected the entire system of that civilization: barbarism and chaos are to be their reward. But Osborne is not a thesis dramatist, carefully preparing each step of an argument to be clinched by the curtain line, and it would be unwise to probe too deeply into the 'meaning' of this final line. *West of Suez*, like the best of Osborne's later work, is a drama whose significance cannot be neatly extracted from the mood which grows out of the apparently insubstantial dialogue.

Both *West of Suez* and *The Hotel in Amsterdam* have a writer as their central figure, and so too does the television play *The Gift of Friendship*. At the beginning of this chapter it was suggested that Osborne has an overriding interest in characters who, whatever their nominal profession, are actors at heart. But George Dillon was a playwright as well as a performer, and the most recent stage of Osborne's career has seemed to show an increasing preoccupation with the creative processes of the writer's craft. (In between, of course, comes *Luther*; Osborne's portrait of the monk's painful search for inspiration reminds us that Luther, too, was a preacher and a writer; and the play is the study of a troubled man's creative powers as much as of specifically 'religious' mentality.) As in other features of his writing, a degree of autobiography is detectable: when he wrote *Epitaph for George Dillon*, Osborne himself was a struggling actor writing during periods of unemployment, whilst *The Hotel in Amsterdam* and *West of Suez* were written by someone familiar with the rewards and demands of literary eminence. But his writers, like his 'actors', have sharply distinctive characters: Wyatt, with his public school background and his affable punditry, is very different from the screen-writer Laurie, vainly trying to escape the attentions of his lower-middle class family in the hectic ambience of the film world.

'Good writers', says Osborne himself, 'are mostly dull dogs'[38]: in *The Gift of Friendship* he comes perilously close to creating a hero who actually is a dull dog. Indeed the writer is, in many ways, the antithesis of the actor: one has the loneliest of professions, the other the most public. The writer develops his craft during long periods of solitude, and can if he chooses remain in the background even when his work is launched upon the public; the actor literally ceases to exist as an artist without the physical presence of an audience. Originality of thought and expression is the *sine qua non* of a writer's personality; the actor must be able to conceal his own individuality behind his interpretation of characters on the stage. But at a deeper level the writer and the actor have much in common. Apart from the critics so detested by Osborne, who thrive like parasites on the creativity of others, the writer, like the actor, is concerned with exploring the feelings, with finding the adequate expression for a particular shade of thought, emotion or experience. The writer works through language and structure; the actor through voice and physical presence; both draw their inspiration, partly from observation of others but also, and much more vitally, from knowledge and honest awareness of themselves and their own experience.

When a creative writer has the personality of an 'actor type', he is far from being a dull dog; he may become, in the words Osborne uses to describe Oscar Wilde, 'his own best creation'[39]. In a sense both Laurie and Wyatt (and indeed, Luther) are 'their own best creations'. When they launch into one of their speeches, one can sense the delight in holding an audience which is one of the features of the 'actor type' and common to most Osborne heroes. But behind that I sense also a deeper element of calculation, of deliberate composition. This is evident enough in the speeches and sermons delivered by Luther; but consider also, for instance, Laurie's parody of the letters he receives from his family, quoted earlier. Despite the triviality of its theme this is a polished, stylish set piece—a little exercise in language which only a born writer would be likely to produce.

Whereas the actor's creative bursts are mostly ephemeral, directed towards performances prepared, delivered and swiftly left behind in the rush of preparation for the next performance, the writer is concerned with a longer time span. The actor remains exclusively in 'Time Present', but the writer's words are enshrined in the permanence of print, and there are few authors who do not at least spare a thought for time past and time future or (to put it another way) are not aware that they exist at a mid-point between the literary tradition which has preceded them and the posterity which, with luck, will accord them a place within that tradition. Earlier in this chapter we have seen how Osborne abandoned his somewhat factitious political concerns as his true talent for presenting a particular consciousness as it displays itself through language developed; in *West of Suez*, it seems to me, he returns to a broader theme. The writer enjoys a 'sense of detachment'; he may live in contemporary society, but his craft brings him continuously into contact with a certain tradition, and by making his central 'actor type' into a writer Osborne has managed to present the scale of values implicit in his idiosyncratic patriotism and his concern for language more organically than in any of his previous works.

Writers who write about writers run the risk of exponentially diminishing returns, and to many critics *West of Suez'* formless successor, *A Sense of Detachment,* did give the impression of a work by someone whose talents were in disintegration. It may be, then, that *West of Suez*, with its sombre picture of a dying culture, marks the end of the road for Osborne. I suspect not, however: someone with his combination of resilient and volatile talents is not likely to be forced into the ultimate refuge of silence. Indeed, since the bulk of this chapter was written, Osborne has completed a further play, *The End of Me Old Cigar.* England in *The Entertainer* was likened to a decaying music hall; in 1975 the metaphorical equivalent has become a brothel run by female militants intent on turning the country's corruption to their own advantage. 'There is in this finely-conceived play a gleam of hope', wrote Harold Hobson, almost alone among critics in liking it[40]. Hobson was referring to the author's hopes for England; whether or not *The End of Me Old Cigar* is a dying ember so far as Osborne's creative powers are concerned, time alone will tell.

Notes to Chapter 2

1 Michael Billington, *The Modern Actor* (London, 1973), Chapter 8
2 *The Modern Actor*, p. 164
3 *The Modern Actor*, Chapter 10
4 p. 60
5 In 'They Call it Cricket', in *Declaration*, ed. Tom Maschler (London, 1957)
6 See for instance Ronald Hayman, *John Osborne* (London, 1968), p. 7
7 *The Plays of John Osborne*, p. 182
8 See especially the Conclusion in *The Plays of John Osborne*, pp. 213ff.
9 See especially 'They Call it Cricket'
10 Most perceptively by John Mander in *The Writer and the Commitment* (London, 1961); the relevant passage is reprinted in John Russell Taylor, ed., *Look Back in Anger: A Casebook* (London, 1968), pp. 143–149
11 See for instance Ronald Hayman, *John Osborne*, p. 48
12 'That Awful Museum', *Twentieth Century* CLXIX (February 1961); reprinted in *Look Back in Anger: A Casebook*, pp. 63–67

13 p. 39

14 p. 14

15 p. 27

16 p. 22

17 'On Critics and Criticism' (*Sunday Telegraph*, 28 August 1966); reprinted in *Look Back in Anger: A Casebook*, pp. 69–71

18 p. 60

19 *The Plays of John Osborne*, pp. 38f

20 *Sunday Times*, 11 May 1956; reprinted in *Look Back in Anger: A Casebook*, p. 47

21 *The Plays of John Osborne*, p. 54

22 p. 38

23 See pp. 32, 72, 87

24 p. 68 (*cf.* p. 84.)

25 *The Plays of John Osborne*, p. 64

26 *Ibid*

27 p. 73

28 p. 28

29 p. 93

30 pp. 139–140

31 p. 132

32 p. 99

33 p. 17

34 p. 52

35 p. 82

36 p. 77

37 p. 74

38 Introduction to *The Picture of Dorian Gray*, p. 12

39 *Ibid*

40 *Sunday Times*, 19 January 1975

3 John Arden: from detachment to anger

'Another frightful ordeal.' With these amiable words Harold Hobson dismissed the first production of *Serjeant Musgrave's Dance*, sparking off one of the earliest of the regular rows between the English Stage Company and the press and plunging Arden into the atmosphere of controversy in which much of his public life has been conducted. *Serjeant Musgrave's Dance* has now achieved its rightful place in contemporary drama, earning respectful mention from the authorities, frequent revivals and the ultimate accolade of becoming an A-level set play. What, then, moved Harold Hobson to his initially bleak response?

It is no coincidence, I think, that whenever one of Ben Jonson's plays is revived Harold Hobson is likely to be less than wholly benign. For Jonson and Arden both write within a tradition that beings with a deeply moral conviction of the social responsibilities of the dramatist. Comedy, declares classical theory, 'holds a mirror up to life', and a mirror, although it may distort, must never lie. For both dramatists, the simple aim of entertaining and giving pleasure is inescapably bound up with the necessity of reflecting, and thus commenting upon, the nature of society. This is what makes both dramatists a minority taste, annoying Harold Hobson into the bargain.

The parallel between Jonson and Arden, in fact, is an extended one[1]. In both cases their view of society is a complicated product of concentrated intellectual energy as much as of the instinctively emotional judgements we have come to expect from our dramatists. They continually surprise us by twists and turns in their argument, exposing a weakness or an ugly side to the hero's nature just as we had confidently invested our sympathy in him, and giving the villains a surprising degree of generous humanity. In Arden's work there is no doubt that this quirkiness becomes exasperating at times: there are occasions when he seems recklessly perverse, and others when he seems as indecisive as the most despised of liberals. But in his best work his refusal to take the obvious stand is always interesting and often a great deal more. Oddly enough, it was Harold Hobson who recognized this quality in *Serjeant Musgrave's Dance*, where other reviewers assumed simply that it was an anti-war play inadequately handled. 'In any case the doctrine that Mr Arden preaches is not comfortable', he wrote, 'least of all to those who imagine that he is unequivocally on their side'[2].

Arden's intellectuality has another consequence, and here too he finds himself in company with the earlier dramatist. Jonson, the learned classicist, was forever exploring the form of comedy and his plays have reached us weighed down with Prologues, Inductions and Dedications explaining precisely what he has borrowed and adapted from the ancient dramatists of Greece and Rome, and the significance of his original contributions to dramatic form. Arden, too, tackles such questions with a wealth of historical knowledge and attention to details of presentation. The differing styles and conventions employed by the dramatists of earlier periods interest Arden immensely: perhaps because of his training as an architect, he has a lively awareness of the limitations of the proscenium arch theatre, and his plays reach the reader prefaced with a variety of suggestions for performance. Unlike John Osborne, whose somewhat casual exploration of dramatic conventions is one of the more superficial aspects of his work, or Harold Pinter, who polishes and perfects his own techniques with little or no conscious reference to tradition, theory or precedent, Arden's approach is (to use that pejorative term) an academic one.

For many writers, some deeply personal event or emotional experience is the mainspring of each new creative work. The bulk of Arden's drama has a somewhat different origin. Events of recent history are seized upon and dramatic equivalents are developed for the moral problems they expose. *Serjeant Musgrave's Dance* is an oblique commentary on a vindictive action taken by British troops during the Cyprus troubles. *Armstrong's Last Goodnight*, dedicated to Conor Cruise O'Brien, draws indirectly upon the history of Katanga's secession from the Congo and the UN's devious involvement. In at least one later play the parallel is somewhat closer. *The Ballygombeen Bequest* claimed to be based upon an actual case-history of attempted eviction by an English landlord near the Ardens' Irish home; after a performance in Belfast it opened at the Edinburgh Festival in 1972, and each night a letter from the author was read from the stage appealing for help and describing the latest developments in that case.

These public themes, refracted through the medium of drama, indicate one side of Arden's commitment to society. There is another side to this commitment, represented by the numerous plays written to fulfill a particular role for a particular occasion or group of people. Even in this respect it is not too farfetched to trace a link with Jonson, whose dramatic works include a series of court masques celebrating the highlights of his monarch's progress through the pages of history as well as the dramas written for the public playhouse. *The Business of Good Government*, a Nativity Play, was written for an amateur group in a Somerset village. *Left-handed Liberty* was commissioned by the City of London to celebrate the 750th anniversary of the signing of the Magna Carta, and presented at the Mermaid Theatre in 1965. Along with his wife Margaretta D'Arcy, Arden was contributing to community and children's theatre long before it had become fashionable. *The Royal Pardon* grew out of a series of bed-time stories the Ardens had made up for their own children, and was presented at the Beaford Arts Centre in Devon in 1966, with John Arden himself in the role of the Constable. *Harold Muggins is a Martyr* was written for performance by amateurs at the left-wing Unity Theatre[3].

Sometimes the combination of *pièce d'occasion* and the social preoccupation becomes peculiarly idiosyncratic. Only John Arden, one feels, could seek to hasten the liberation of the English stage from the shackles of censorship with a one-act play (*The True History of Squire Jonathan*

51

and his Unfortunate Treasure, presented at a lunch-time theatre club in 1968) which unites the celebration of total nudity with an obscure allegory on the nature of wealth, and call the whole result an 'autobiographical play'.

It was inevitable, I suppose, that such an author (or to be accurate, pair of authors, since most of Arden's recent work has been written in collaboration with his wife) should end up at loggerheads with the structure and organization of the contemporary theatre. As is natural in a dramatist whose artistic principles go hand in hand with his social convictions, Arden's objection to the theatre is partly aesthetic, partly political.

Early in his career Arden established a reputation as an 'uncommitted' writer, warily anxious not to simplify the complexities of human motivation to make a political point, and along with this went a refusal to preach. 'I am not normally an enthusiast for didactic drama', he wrote in the Notes to *Left-Handed Liberty*[4]. In time this 'uncommitted' stance has moved closer and closer to the revolutionary viewpoint of the radical left, and, (as might be expected) the further Arden has moved to the left, the less cautious he has been about avoiding the perils of didacticism. Partly, it is no secret, this change of direction has been due to the influence of his wife ('And she is Irish and most radical', he declares[5]; and a visit to India in 1970, when he experienced the poverty and deprivation of the Third World at first hand, undoubtedly strengthened his sympathies. It was a new Arden who wrote (in 1971):

> ... I recognize as the enemy the fed man, the clothed man, the sheltered man, whose food, clothes, and house are obtained at the expense of the hunger, the nakedness, and the exposure of so many millions of others: and who will allow anything to be *said*, in books or on the stage, so long as the food, clothes, and house remain undiminished in his possession[6].

Roughly speaking, the further Arden has moved to the left, the more impatient he has become of the shortcomings of the established theatre. The National Theatre's lavish revival of *Armstrong's Last Goodnight* in 1965 (it was first presented by the Glasgow Citizens' Theatre in the previous year) was the last production by a major subsidized company at which public harmony reigned. The circumstances surrounding the first night of *The Hero Rises Up*, the next play to be entrusted to a subsidized company in London, when it was presented by the Institute of Contemporary Arts at the Round House in 1968, are described by the authors:

> While we were producing the play we became involved in a quarrel with our management, the ICA. They had to *do things properly*, being responsible to their responsibilities ... and as the audience assembled we stood in the foyer like a pair of vexed Picts, committing what in my childhood was the prime social crime of the lower middle-class suburb where I lived—we were 'Brawling on the Doorstep' with the managerial representatives.   (p. 6)

The production of *The Island of the Mighty* by the Royal Shakespeare Company in 1972 led to an even sharper dispute, in which the authors eventually disowned the production with the claim that 'among other things, the meaning of the play had been crucially shifted out of balance, producing an imperialistic effect alien to our original intentions"[7]. As members of the Irish Society of Playwrights they declared themselves on strike, and for a day or two journalists were able to report on the sorry spectacle of the Ardens picketing the theatre where their play was in rehearsal.

One might conclude that the Ardens are naturally quarrelsome, but that this has nothing to do with the quality of their plays. In fact their disputes with officialdom do, it seems to me, throw an interesting light on their drama. In the course of their 'Asymmetrical Authors' Preface' the Ardens develop an explanation of their dispute with the ICA over *The Hero Rises Up* that is so eccentric it hardly seems to be intended seriously. The moment when they stood in the foyer 'like a couple of vexed Picts' is nothing less than a legacy of the Roman invasion of Britain. The Romans, they explain, were determined to improve everything:

> . . . and the improvement was to be carried out with symmetry and efficiency, and, above all, *done properly*. The native Celts never entirely submitted. Then the Romans left us: and the English arrived. . . . Eventually they conquered these natives, despising them for their comparative lack of power, and—by extension—for their 'curvilinear' asymmetry. (p. 5)

The old battle between the curvilinear Celts and the symmetrical Romans, intent on having everything 'done properly', was still being fought on that fateful opening night. Curious as it seems, this argument holds the key to much of Arden's work, including the earliest, 'uncommitted' plays. The Roman and Anglo-Saxon principles of good order, discipline and efficiency are treated by Arden with a healthy disrespect; he sees them as prosaic, oppressive forces and sides instinctively with the old Celtic and 'British' nature, its subtle and ingenious minds, its fondness for devious activity and oblique poetry, and its ready diversion from the line of duty to follow the call of hospitality or the allure of a fair woman.

Not for nothing has Arden throughout his working life been preoccupied with the figure of Arthur, the last British king. 'This Island has been called by her poets "The Island of the Mighty"', declares Arthur to his British troops as they prepare for final battle against the English[8], and Arden in a very real sense is the dramatist of the Island of the Mighty, with its old unruly civilisation of poetry and wild religion as remote from London and its orderly ways of government as are the moors and isolated townships of his native Yorkshire.

In most of Arden's work, therefore, there is a vital tension between the public man, soberly drawing his balanced portraits of society, and the private poet with his quick, intuitive sympathies that mock law and order at every turn. There is an astonishingly wide choice of subject-matter in Arden's plays, ranging from a panoramic treatment of the last years of ancient Britain to portraits of contemporary small-town politics, and from a dramatisation of the nativity to a relentless attack upon absentee landlords. But behind this diversity there lies a remarkably consistent collection of interests and sympathies, and in this section I shall try to point to a few outstanding landmarks along the way.

Stylistically, Arden's use of verse set him apart from his fellows in the English theatre of the 1950s. The previous generation of dramatists had included Eliot and Fry, and for a time the hopes of the ailing English theatre had been pinned to the prospect of a revival of poetic drama. But Fry and Eliot, both Christian in religion and conservative in temperament, had no followers of any stature, and indeed by the late 1950s, in the face of the angry emotionalism of an Osborne or a Wesker, their poetry had come to seem more of a restricting than a liberating force. Arden found a new place for verse in the theatre, using it in a way that owes something to Brecht, something to the English ballad tradition, and a great deal to his own sense of the poet's role within society.

I have referred to Arden as a moral dramatist, and so he is; but his morality is a very curious one by everyday modern standards. It is in part, I suspect, the moral code of a bardic society, which the Greece of Homer or the Britain of Taliesin might have recognized, but not the centrally organized, bureaucratic administration of the Roman Empire or its later English counterpart. It is a kind of linguistic morality in which events and emotions have a second existence, at least as important as their first, when they are captured and preserved in the memorable phrases of the poet. Arden's prescription for the use of verse in his own plays gives some indication of this:

> The ancient Irish heroic legends were told at dinner as prose tales, of invariable content but, in the manner of their telling, improvised to suit the particular occasion of the poet's mood. When, however, he arrived at one of the emotional climaxes of the story such as the lament of Deirdre for the Sons of Usna or the sleep-song of Grainne over Diarmaid, then he would sing a poem which he had by heart and which was always the same. So in a play, the dialogue can be naturalistic and 'plotty' as long as the basic poetic issue has not been crystallized. But when this point is reached, then the language becomes formal (if you like, in verse, or sung), the visual pattern coalesces into a vital image that is one of the nerve-centres of the play[9].

We are used to the idea of Arden as a poet; it is worth remembering that his prose too is often remarkable. In the pages that follow sufficient examples will be quoted to show that he is not only a writer of vigorous, precisely organized prose, but a fully dramatic writer adapting his style to meet each new character. In this passage from Arden's first full-length play *The Waters of Babylon* Krank (a prototype of the Krank we met in *Wet Fish*) is following his daily habit of changing from the scruffy clothes he wears at home into the dark businessman's suit he dons by day to work in an architect's office:

> Baker Street Station. Here is that extremely convenient arrangement, a gentlemen's convenience with a door at either end of it. A most remarkable, and, I think, beautiful phenomenon. I am about to be reborn: in this twentieth-century peculiar ceremonial womb, glazed tiles and electric light beneath the golden pavement stones of London, hygienic underground renascence, for *me*, is daily routine.   (p. 28)

Krank, with his polite irony and his somewhat curious word-order, is every inch a central European making himself at home in a foreign city and a foreign language (and Krank's elaborate sartorial exchange, as we shall see, is an introduction in a minor key to one of Arden's themes: costumes, uniforms and insignia of all kinds are a vital part of his dramatic shorthand, indicating at a glance the social role of his characters, while at the same time his vivid sense of the contrast between the figure presented to the outside world and the naked man beneath prevents it from becoming a merely mechanical device).

Alas, Arden's dramatic prose is of variable quality. The closer he gets to naturalism the less happy his gift for words. Even his rogues and vagabonds draw on a vocabulary which is not in the least realistic, but carefully though imaginatively compiled from a variety of sources, oral and literary. Setting dialogue of this kind of polished artificiality into the structure of the play as a whole sometimes turns out a chancy business. Also from *The Waters of Babylon*, in this passage two of Krank's adjutants are comparing notes. They have been meeting immigrants off the boat trains (Bathsheba deals with her fellow West Indians, and Cassidy is Irish); never can the sordid business of inveigling innocent girls into a life of prostitution have been expressed in such exuberant language:

BATHSHEBA: Two today from Trinidad and there was one from Jamaica. Not what I'd call real proud-jetting young women, not what I'd call flying fish or torpedoes. No sir, just kind of sad and quiet gentle sea-weed laid out dark on a hard cold beach. You've been along to meet a train too?

CASSIDY: The Irish Mail, no less. And there they stepped down from it, six beautiful doxies. Sea-weed?—No sea-weed but all roaring gorse, wild whitethorn, a chiming tempest of girls, turned that Euston station into a true windswept altitude, a crystal mountain-top for love. Or for Mr Krank's finances, which is more to the bloody purpose. (p. 42)

Some dramatists have difficulty in convincing us that their characters are as intelligent as they are supposed to be; Arden, like Congreve, has the reverse problem and finds difficulty in showing us a slow brain sluggishly converting dull thoughts into words. We sometimes wonder how one Arden character can ever be outwitted by another, they all seem so clever. Similarly, Bathsheba and Cassidy seem to be carrying a weight of linguistic skill far beyond their station in life, even within the far from naturalistic conventions of *The Waters of Babylon*.

As we argued in Chapter 1, Arden is a dramatist interested in society. This is certainly reflected in the language and imagery of his characters, who are always keenly aware of rank and role, and it emerges still more clearly in the passages of verse, with their generalizing quality; but it is of course in the structure of his plays that this side of Arden's character as a writer is most clearly expressed. To say that Arden is interested in society is only an approximation, for Arden is certainly no sociologist, writing of average people and common experience. Rather, he sees society as a fluid, reciprocal relationship between individuals and the community. In abstract terms, this gives his drama a distinctly Brechtian flavour: his audiences must avoid complete involvement with the characters on stage, or they will miss the larger pattern. But whatever techniques Arden may have in common with Brecht, the world-picture that emerges from his plays is distinctly his own.

As John Russell Taylor has shown in his introduction to Arden's first three published plays[10], any play by Arden is likely to contain, not one community or group of people, but two at least, each with a private code of values incompatible with anyone else's, and each displaying a human mixture of virtues and vices. At some point the fragile relationship between the two communities is disturbed, and disaster threatens. As we discovered in *Wet Fish*, Arden likes to explore the limits of a stable society, showing how the established balance (which usually has little to do with our own conventional notions of legality or morality) can be tipped in the direction of chaos by an action offending the secret code which binds the whole together. Although, as is often pointed out, Arden distributes good qualities and bad among his characters and thus avoids commitment in any simple sense, he has a heart; and in most of his plays one can tell where it lies. It is quite obvious, for instance, that he likes Krank in *The Waters of Babylon*, although he exploits his tenants and, worse still, lures innocent girls into a life of shame. Krank gets most of the best lines in the play and, for that matter, most of the girls as well. In *Live Like Pigs* it is the roistering Sawneys, with their petty pilfering and their free-and-easy promiscuity, who have sympathetic treatment, while Arden's depiction of their new neighbours the Jacksons, clinging primly to new-found respectability, often borders upon simple caricature.

To summarize Arden's attitude towards social and legal morality, one might suggest that there is a huge difference in his world between *breaking the rules* and *overstepping the mark*. Rules are there to be broken, as part and parcel of what I have suggested Arden sees as the Roman, Anglo-Saxon world of regulation and intolerance, and the best part of life lies somewhere in the uncharted area beyond these rules, where right and wrong has to be determined instinctively; and it is in this area that Arden's intelligence and originality sets most enthusiastically to work.

Within this framework, recurrent characters emerge. In his 'autiobiographical play' *The Bagman*, broadcast in 1970, the Narrator, who quickly reveals himself as

> John Arden (thirty-eight) of ancient family,
> Writer of plays for all the world to see . . .   (p. 37)

describes his adventures in a dream-world full of symbols pointing to the author's own progress through troubled times. His sole possession is an old army kit-bag, acquired mysteriously from an aged gipsy-woman, which he discovers to be full of 'little men and little women'—carefully constructed animated puppets, 'each one of them dressed in a characteristic costume':

> . . . there was a Soldier in a red coat, and a Policeman, and a Doctor with great spectacles, and a pretty little blonde Popsy and a blowsy soot-stained Housewife with a baby at her breast, and a hideous Old Woman, and a Robber with a great sword and bushy whiskers . . .   (p. 57)

Between them, these little people form a kind of repertory company capable of appearing in the major roles of most Arden plays. Policemen, for instance, tread their way regularly through his drama (they have not been altogether absent from his personal life, as the Dedication and Introduction to *Two Autobiographical Plays* make clear). In his two earliest stage plays order is restored by the police in the final scenes, while in *Serjeant Musgrave's Dance* the providential arrival of a troop of Dragoons performs the same task. There is a memorable comic policeman in the children's play *The Royal Pardon* (played by Arden himself in the first production), and in *The Workhouse Donkey* the incorruptible Colonel Feng's attempts to impose a policeman's law and order upon a northern town is the mainspring of the plot. Policemen are important figures in Arden's plays, I think, because with the unrelieved black of their uniforms and the humourless precision of their world-view they are the embodiment not so much of Justice as of the Rules, the inescapable shadow of Roman Law.

Another character who has clearly fascinated Arden is the Soldier. Like the policeman his function is proclaimed by his costume, but he is more colourful and at the same time more enigmatic. Arden has an ambiguous attitude towards the swaggering, uniformed adventurer who knows no laws and yet is ruled by an iron discipline. This theme, of course, lies at the heart of *Serjeant Musgrave's Dance*; and *Soldier, Soldier*, Arden's first play for television, is a rather less successful study of the same figure. Several years later Luke in *The Royal Pardon*, a children's play with a far from childish theme, provides a fascinating study of the paradox of the warrior, the most attractive of individuals harnessed to the cruellest sort of human conduct.

The policeman represents violence contained within society, while the soldier's violence exists outside the social norm, subject to its own fierce code of military honour. The causes and effects of violence, as any study of Arden's plays will reveal, are a topic of perennial fascination to him; but he is also interested in its opposite. The person who can get what he wants by skilful manipulation of other people's self-interest has no need of the policeman's truncheon or the soldier's sword: the devious ways of the intriguer form another of Arden's major themes. It emerges in his first play *The Waters of Babylon*, when Krank teams up with one Charles Butterthwaite (an older, run-down version of the mighty Butterthwaite who soars to his proper height in *The Workhouse Donkey*) in an ill-fated plot to capture the prize from a local municipal lottery. As the playwright's work develops this interest in intrigue is often painted on to a broader canvas, so that it becomes a political study in the nature of diplomacy; and the skilful politician, another of Arden's characteristic figures, enters his drama. Arden's favourite historical characters are not Churchillian personages thundering their way to fame, but more resourceful individuals who through the exercise of their wits manipulate forces much stronger than their own.

The first of these calculating politicans is Herod in the nativity play *The Business of Good Government*. Arden's Herod is far from being the raging, blustering monster of the medieval drama which provides the ultimate model for this play; instead, he becomes an astute figure who demonstrates the finite quality of political morality: Arden shows how an intelligent ruler of 'a small country in a very dangerous position' would inevitably interpret the miraculous rumours circulating in his

Kingdom as a threat to the regime, and act accordingly. King John in *Left-Handed Liberty*, Arden's eccentric celebration of the 750th anniversary of Magna Carta, is a similar sort of ruler, playing off his barons against one another in a devious power-game; later in this chapter we shall see more of two plays in which diplomacy plays a vital part, *Armstrong's Last Goodnight* and *The Island of the Mighty* with its massive cast of Kings and poet-strategists.

This summary by no means exhausts the list of Arden's favourite characters: like many intellectuals, he allows his mind to dwell from time to time on the attractive properties of lascivious woman-kind: among the puppets in *The Bagman* we find

> ... this bright-eyed Girl, her bum
> Round as an apple or a plum.
> She is any girl who will lie down
> Whether for love or half-a-crown ...   (p. 59)

There is no poet among the 'little men' in *The Bagman*, but the central character is a dramatist in crisis, and not least among Arden's major characters there stands the poet or artist. To many people's way of thinking the artist is someone who withdraws from society to explore an aesthetic world of strictly private sensibilities; Arden, by contrast, sees the poet as another public figure contributing as much to the social framework as the policeman or the politician.

Ars Longa, Vita Brevis, the Ardens' wayward contribution to the RSC Theatre of Cruelty season, is an early skirmish with the subject of the artist in society. The new art master appointed to St Uncumbers attracts the decidedly unprogressive headmaster because of his firm view on curriculum discipline: 'No free expression', he promises. His first class shows him insisting on the use of 'straight lines':

> With your rulers, and your T-squares, no freehand, no expressionism, impressionism, futurism, abstractism... No laxity, keep to purity of the forms, the line is rigid ...   (p. 15)

'Everything sharp sharp sharp as the point of a bayonet', he demands, and before long the militaristic fury of his craving for discipline drives him into the Territorial Army where he meets his end in a shooting accident. His wife's lament is ambiguous:

> I shed a tear upon his bier
> Because to me he was ever dear.
> But I could not follow him in all his wishes
> I prefer the quick easy swimming of the fishes
> Which sport and play
> In green water all day
> And have not a straight line in the whole of their bodies.   (p. 20)

The covert relationship between discipline and violence, stability and freedom, the opposing roles of the artist and the soldier, emerge unsystematically in this loosely structured work like obsessions revealed on the psychoanalyst's couch during a free association session. They are somewhat curiously linked by the metaphor of the 'straight line': but time after time, in Arden's geometry, it is a 'straight line' that proves the shortest road to damnation.

Ars Longa, Vita Brevis presents an artist who becomes a soldier, with tragicomic results; the hero of *The Royal Pardon* is a soldier who becomes an actor, with much happier consequences. It may be a children's play but Luke, a fugitive from the 'recent wars in Flanders' is no toy soldier, as this typical snatch of Arden minstrelsy reveals:

> Starving though we were and tired and ill
> We never did forget our soldier's skill:
> We kept our boots clean and our bayonets bright,
> We waved our banners and we marched upright,
> We dared the French to meet us and to fight.
> And when we met we fought till none could stand.
> Our bodies now lie in a foreign land,
> Defeated, they have said. But we know better:
> We obeyed our general's orders to the letter.   (pp. 52–53)

He falls in love with the strolling actress Esmeralda and saves the day when her company, performing at a royal wedding, is nearly put out of action by the rival French team. The princely accolade which eventually greets the itinerant actors has little appeal for Luke. While Mr and Mrs Croke, the booming professional tragedians who lead the company, accept a contract as 'players to the Royal Household', Luke and Esmeralda politely take their leave:

> Therefore it you're willing, we will say our fond good-byes.
> Take yourselves off to London, act before the king:
> We two will attempt together a far more dangerous thing.
> We will travel, hand in hand,
> Across water and dry land—
> We will entertain the people
> Under castle-wall and proud church steeple . . .   (p. 107)

Life, as Oscar Wilde sagely observed, has a habit of imitating Art; when we reflect that in an earlier scene the Crokes had thoroughly mangled their dramatic treatment of the story of Arthur and Merlin, *The Royal Pardon* turns out to be an uncannily accurate forecast of the upset between the Ardens themselves and the Royal Shakespeare Company over *The Island of the Mighty*: Luke and Esmeralda's 'fond good-byes' to the lavishly subsidized royal players anticipate the Ardens' own rejection of the institutional theatre of the 1970s.

Arden's poets tend to be public men, involved in affairs of state. In *Armstrong's Last Goodnight* the King's circuitous diplomat Lindsay is described as 'ane very pleasureable contriver . . . of farces, ballads, allegories, and the like delights of poetry . . . ane man of rhetoric and discrete humanity'. And in *The Island of the Mighty* the relationship of the poet to the public life of the community forms one of the principal themes. In his 'Author's Preface' Arden describes how he came to view Arthur's chief poet Merlin as a type of the 'liberal intellectual who no longer knows what is liberality and what is tyranny, who is unable to draw a distinction between poetic ambiguity and political dishonesty . . .'—in short, a poet with a catalogue of confusing characteristics not unlike those of Arden himself[11].

Arden, as has already been mentioned, shows a progressive impatience with the ways of the conventional theatre; as early as *The*

Workhouse Donkey he declared that he would have been happy for the play 'to have lasted, say, six or seven or thirteen hours', with the audience coming and going in a theatre with 'some of the characteristics of a fairground or amusement park, with restaurants, bars, sideshows, bandstands and so on'. The theatre, he declared, must 'grant pride of place to the old essential attributes of Dionysus'[12]. By the time the Ardens wrote *The Hero Rises Up* this had become a plea for a kind of drama 'which need not be *done properly*'. The Ardens had developed a concept of theatre similar to Peter Brook's definition of 'rough theatre'. Brook describes this (somewhat romantically) as:

> ... the theatre that's not in a theatre, the theatre on carts, on wagons, on trestles, audiences standing, drinking, sitting round tables, audiences joining in, answering back[13].

Perhaps the first full-length play in which this kind of technique is successfully exploited by the Ardens is *The Royal Pardon*. Written for children and never presented in London, it has not had the attention it deserves, for it contains a good deal of the Ardens' writing at its best. Luke is one of the most fully-developed of Arden's soldier figures, touching in simple, appropriate language upon the ambiguities surrounding the man who makes a career of war, while the final discovery of his true vocation as an actor 'under castle-wall and proud church steeple' is a happy coincidence of the play's theme and the Ardens' own intentions.

Rough theatre, at any rate for the Ardens, does not mean imprecise theatre. In *The Royal Pardon* the language is robust, yet exact, and despite its pantomime qualities the plot has all the complicated hallmarks of Arden's drama. Cutting across the intrigue and politicking surrounding the two teams of actors competing for royal favour there is another pattern of mutual attraction between the sexes; and through it all plods the Constable on the track of Luke, a humorous version of *The Workhouse Donkey's* Feng, the zealous officer of the law who nearly upsets the delicate balance between the two groups.

The Ardens' next major venture was *The Hero Rises Up*, the play which caused so much trouble with the ICA. It is sub-titled 'A Romantic Melodrama' and extends the 'rough theatre' techniques of *The Royal Pardon* into the world of adult drama. The hero of the title is Lord Nelson, and the play is a characteristically double-edged study of an expert in the art of warfare. Written with the panache of a Victorian melodrama, it presents scenes from Nelson's life in a series of *tableaux vivants*, each with its significant action proclaimed on a placard. The dialogue is strong and rhetorical, and intended for musical accompaniment (the original meaning of 'melodrama'); like the action it demands exaggeration rather than subtlety. Behind all the bustle, alas, one detects a certain aimlessness, and the Ardens' examination of the myths surrounding the great naval commander eventually leaves everyone a little at sea.

In fact towards the end of the 1960s Arden, along with many other intellectuals of broadly liberal sympathies, seems to have entered a period of uncertainty if not of actual crisis. Fortunately for us, the outcome was his remarkable autobiographical play *The Bagman*. It opens with a rueful Arden surveying his limited achievements so far. If he dropped dead 'on this soggy Thursday', he reflects, there would not be much to be said for him:

> He covered yards of stage-cloth with invented people,
> He worked alone for years yet was not able
> To chase one little rat from underneath the table.   (p. 38)

In the dream-world he enters after falling asleep on a park bench he relives the excitement of the discovery of his abilities as a dramatist, symbolized by the 'little men':

> Laugh and leap or shake with terror,
> My little men will be your mirror.
> What you do or what you did
> From little people can't be hid:
> They will know it and reflect
> In strut and jerk your every act—
> Your thoughts expressed in dark of night
> They body forth in broad daylight.   (p. 58)

But, as his understanding of the injustices of society around him increases—helped along by a Young Woman who has enticed him into her bed, and initiated some post-coital political instruction—his creative powers flag. His lover proclaims the coming revolution and somewhat desperately he 'dedicates' his little men to the cause. They prove uncooperative:

> ... they were all clustering and huddling together, some of them struggling to get back into the bag ... What are you doing—why do you not respond to me—you have your business to perform—for God's sake get on with it—would you put me to shame before all these men of war?   (p. 85)

After this point, with the revolution on the brink of betrayal, the narrator wakes up near Highgate Underground Station. Homeward bound, he contemplates the dramatist's inability to do anything substantial to help the deprived and dispossessed:

> Such is not my nature, nor will be.
> All I can do is to look at what I see ...   (p. 88)

The Bagman was written in 1969, before the Ardens' visit to India; in the Preface which was written after their return Arden insists 'the attitude of the central character at the end of the story is reprehensible, cowardly, and not to be imitated'. Between the Arden of 1969 and the Arden of 1971 there lies a clearly discernible gulf; in the concluding section of this Chapter we shall see how it has worked its effect on the most recent of the Ardens' plays.

The most remarkable scene in *Serjeant Musgrave's Dance* comes towards the end of the play when Musgrave, ostensibly a recruiting sergeant, but in fact a crazed deserter intent on making his own protest against the horror of colonial war, calls a meeting in the town square of a Northern mining village, levels a Gatling gun at the spectators and hoists aloft not the patriotic flag but the skeleton, still in a soldier's tunic, of a boy who had left the town to joint the army. As Musgrave performs his dance, 'waving his rifle, his face contorted with demoniac fury', there is a moment when music, language and stage spectacle unite in a theatrical moment of undeniable power[15]. But even here Arden does the unexpected; for the dance is not the conclusion of the scene, but rather the inauguration of a detailed analysis of Musgrave's frantic philosophy. For another fifteen pages Musgrave argues and pleads, losing the support first of Attercliffe and then of the colliers themselves as his willingness to use violence for his own ends becomes apparent, until the providential arrival of a troop of Dragoons puts paid to his schemes. If the play were simply a protest against war, this might seem like mismanagement; but as I shall argue, that is not quite the case.

Two main criticisms were levelled against the play when it first appeared. The first was that the characters were not explored in sufficient depth. They 'never get a chance to develop', complained A. Alvarez; 'they have simple purposes but no complexity of life, like so many puppets[16]'. A fair judge would admit that Alvarez's comment is not entirely baseless. The puppets in *The Bagman* had a certain independence of their master, it will be recalled, but the characters in *Serjeant Musgrave's Dance* are sometimes puppets in a more conventional sense. They fulfil their theatrical role in the machinery of the play obediently enough: like most of Arden's characters they fall into two major groups, the soldiers apparently on a recruiting campaign but actually deserters whom Musgrave has pressed into service for his enterprise, and the townsmen in a mining village where an industrial dispute is coming to a head. A few characters belong to neither group: the officer of Dragoons, an impersonal figure who restores the order with his troops, the two women at the inn where the soldiers lodge, and the interesting figure of Joe Bludgeon, the bargee who ferries the soldiers along the canal to the town. They are sharply and effectively differentiated; where Arden seems to me to fail in comparison with his later work is in the isolation which these characters suffer. It is natural of course that Musgrave should be separated from the others by his deluded mind; but nowhere in the play is there, for instance, anything corresponding to the friendship between Sir David Lindsay and his secretary in *Armstrong's Last Goodnight* or the good-humoured badinage of the Labour councillors in *The Workhouse Donkey*. The few deft touches which integrate a character into his human surroundings and convert an analysis of a society into the portrayal of a community are missing in *Serjeant Musgrave's Dance*.

Equally vigorous among the first reactions to the play were the objections raised against the plot. Bernard Levin's review sums up the exasperation of his fellow-critics: 'Why is it fully one and a half acts before we have any idea of what is going on?' he asked. 'The suspicion grows that Mr Arden actually regards clarity and directness as vices.'[17] In that last sentence, of course, Bernard Levin was almost right. There is clarity, of a strange sort, in most of Arden's work, but directness is an Anglo-Saxon virtue he rarely admits into his drama. One natural conclusion, on a first encounter with the play, is that it is about war and the evils of war, and on this view the earlier part of the play does indeed appear as little more than an unduly extended exposition leading to Musgrave's wild action in the town square. But *Serjeant Musgrave's Dance* is not so much a play about war as about violence in more general terms, and still more it is a play about discipline, repression and anarchy. It may be true, as Ronald Hayman points out[18], that Arden handles the revelation of the true nature of Musgrave's mission rather clumsily in the first act, but Act II has a much tighter structure. In the first scene Musgrave begins his 'recruiting campaign' by entertaining local colliers to free drinks. Tension is already running high in the town on account of the strike and consequent lockout, and when the Constable tries to clear the bar at closing time an ugly fight develops. Attercliffe, the oldest of the three soldiers, is left 'trembling all over':

> ATTERCLIFFE: He was going to, Serjeant. He would have, he'd killed him. It's always here. Kill him. Kill.
> MUSGRAVE: [*roughly*]: That'll do . . . We've all had enough, Mr Constable. I'll get this lot to bed. (p. 47)

To Musgrave, the incident is simply an irritating threat to his plans; to Attercliffe it is a disturbing reminder of the violence he has renounced. Inevitably, as the soldiers bed down for the night Annie, whose mind has been disturbed since her lover went to war, is amongst them, and Attercliffe, trying to prevent a squabble for her favours between the other two, finds himself unwittingly the killer of Sparky, the youngest and most innocent of the group. Musgrave presses grimly on with his self-imposed task:

> ATTERCLIFFE: Musgrave, what are you doing?
> MUSGRAVE: I'm doing what comes next and that's all I've got time for.
> ATTERCLIFFE: [*in a gush of despair*]: But he was killed, you see, killed. Musgrave, don't you see, that wipes the whole thing out, wiped out, washed out, finished.
> MUSGRAVE: *No!* (p. 73)

It is clear that a pattern of outbursts of vindictive violence is foreshadowing Musgrave's account of the night the troops lost control in the next act. It is not war, but the human proneness to wild violence, and the fragility of our self-control, which lies at the heart of this act.

At the centre of it all is the figure of Black Jack Musgrave, tense, determined, brushing aside every obstacle with the words 'It's not material'. In many ways he is an archetypal illustration of Arden's belief in the perils of the logic of 'straight lines'. Earlier in this chapter I suggested that the difference between breaking the rules and overstepping the mark was important to Arden: Musgrave is someone who adheres rigidly to the rules he has invented, and ends by overstepping the mark with spectacular frenzy. The audience receives its first hint that Musgrave is unhinged when he delivers his prayer at the conclusion of Act I:

> All my life a soldier I've made You prayers and made them straight, I've reared my one true axe against the timber and I've launched it true. My regiment was my duty, and I called Death honest, killing by the book—but it all got scrawled and mucked about and I could not think clear . . . Now I have my duties different. I'm in this town to change all soldiers' duties. (p. 37)

Musgrave's madness is made plainer, if by a somewhat hackneyed device, in the next act as he cries out involuntarily in his sleep, evidently reliving some terrible event[19]; what that event was we discover in Act III when, in a long, vivid speech beneath the dangling skeleton, he recounts how five innocent lives were taken in reprisal for his comrade's death. But he goes beyond the plan he had outlined to Attercliffe and the others:

> You see, the Queen's Book, which eighteen years I've lived, it's turned inside out for *me*. There used to be my duty: now there's a disease—   (p. 90)

Attercliffe shows some alarm, but Musgrave presses inexorably on:

> One man, and for him five. Therefore, for five of them we multiply out, *and* we find it five-and-twenty ... So, as I understand Logic and Logic to me is the mechanism of God—that means that today there's twenty-five persons will have to be—   (p. 91)

The confusion that follows seems likely to end in general bloodshed when, conveniently on cue, the Dragoons sent for by the Mayor as a precaution against rioting arrive, a courteous officer places Musgrave under arrest, and 'law and order is established'[20].

The suspicion that behind the public play about the nature of war and violence there lies a more individual exploration of private themes is confirmed by a study of the figure of the bargee. In some ways, one feels, the plot could do very well without him; but a closer examination of the play's texture reveals how important he is to Arden's scheme of things. He is involved in every major scene; unlike the others, whose actions are single-minded expressions of their predetermined role, he owes allegiance to nothing and no-one and behaves with unshackled mischievousness. At one moment he is earning the price of a drink by suggesting to the Parson that the recruiting party may be 'useful' in the strike-torn town; next he is suggesting to Walsh, the most dangerous of the striking colliers, that the Gatling gun brought by the recruiting party could help his cause; and when a party led by Walsh does break into the improvised armoury, it is the bargee who is the first to warn Musgrave. He is the only one to show any sort of support for Musgrave's insane appeal to the people: 'I'm with you, general!' he cries. Yet when the Dragoons arrive he seizes a rifle and thrusts it into Musgrave's back[21]. The bargee is a kind of antidote to Musgrave's world-view: while Musgrave obeys the rules of Logic—'and Logic to me is the mechanism of God'—and marches rigidly into black insanity, crooked Joe Bludgeon breaks all the rules in the book and eventually restores a kind of health to the community. We see him mocking Musgrave at prayer, parodying the parade-ground antics of the military[22], and finally, when Musgrave has been placed under arrest, he hands out the free beer brought by the serjeant and leads a dance around the town-square in which coal-owners and strikers, the Constable and even the rebellious Walsh, join to wash away the memory of Serjeant Musgrave's dance.

The Workhouse Donkey contains many of Arden's characteristic preoccupations, jostling against each other in some confusion. In this play the two major groups of characters are formed by the Labour and Conservative councillors of a contemporary north-country town: one of Arden's major successes lies in the way he presents this enormous community (the cast list runs to two whole pages) with its interlocking interests, balancing the public, political role of the characters against a credible protrayal of their human characteristics. Their easy-going public morality is overseen by a local police force which keeps an indulgent eye on things; trouble begins when a new Chief Constable is appointed, determined to stamp out crime and corruption wherever he may come across it. In Colonel Feng we have another of Arden's straight-backed supporters of Anglo-Saxon morality, in this case the very embodiment of Law and Order. His unswerving rectitude soon comes into conflict with the local life-style: Councillor Butterthwaite, for instance, is in the habit of convening committee meetings in the local pub after closing time, while Sweetman, his Tory rival, has financial interests in a drinking club outside town which is not too scrupulous about observing the strict terms of its licence. Both sides try to enlist Feng's aid for political ends, and the conflict escalates to the point where the cheerful breaking of the rules goes too far, and Butterthwaite is blackmailed into robbing the council-house safe.

A major theme of the play is broached when Feng falls in love with the oddly named Wellesley Blomax who, as the daughter of someone involved in the crime he is investigating, occasions a critical conflict between his heart and his principles. Or rather, it should: unfortunately neither Wellesley nor Feng are likely to convince the most sympathetic of audiences that their exchange of pleasantries over cream cakes in the municipal tea gardens is love as we know it, and the lack of emotional credibility in this section of the play is an undeniable weakness.

Feng finally admits defeat and heads back south to the world he understands, but the overthrow of law and order is by no means the only element in the plot, however much revolves around it. If Feng corresponds to some extent to Black Jack Musgrave, as a man whose obedience to his own principles brings about his downfall, the Bargee has his equivalent in Dr Wellington Blomax (father of Wellesley): like Feng, he is from the south and attached to neither of the groups within the play, but like the Bargee he is devoid of moral scruples and he wins our sympathies despite his deplorable behaviour. Arden makes him a kind of ironic narrator, stepping in and out of the action and manipulating it to suit his own devious purposes; but he in his turn is manipulated when he is persuaded to pressure Butterthwaite, the workhouse donkey of the title, into burgling the council to repay a gambling debt. The actual robbery is one of the highlights of the play, carried out by Butterthwaite in pantomime style as he sings an autobiographical ditty:

> In the workhouse I was born
> On one Christmas day
> Two long ears and four short feet
> And all I ate was hay.
>
> Hay for breakfast, hay for dinner
> Lovely hay for tea,
> I thank my benefactors thus
> Hee-haw hee-haw *hee*!   (p. 99)

Butterthwaite is a character who succeeds in unbalancing the play, towering above his fellow councillors on either side of the political fence. The final scene, in which he breaks up a decorous gathering celebrating

the opening of a new art gallery, has an Aristophanic ring about it.
Surrounded by admiring supporters and garlanded with flowers, he
helps himself to champagne and scornfully takes his leave:

> Out he goes the poor old donkey
> Out he goes in rain and snow,
> For to make the house place whiter
> Who will be the next to go?

(p. 130)

Arden may be a social dramatist, but he is not a very economic one. The
plot of *The Workhouse Donkey* sprawls unmanageably, sometimes hit-
ting its target, sometimes missing; Butterthwaite, memorable and
magnificent though he is, leaves one wondering about his role. Ronald
Hayman likens him to Goetz in *Ironhand* and Gilnockie in *Armstrong's
Last Goodnight*, as an anachronism whose anarchic approach to life is
stifled by encroaching order[23]. But Butterthwaite, one feels, would have
been an anachronism whenever he had lived. *The Workhouse Donkey* is
subtitled 'A Vulgar Melodrama', and Arden's expressed desire for a
riotous entertainment that goes beyond the boundaries of normal
theatrical experience is partially achieved through Butterthwaite in the
robbery scene and the finale, but is at odds with the observation of small-
town corruption (akin to the theme in *Wet Fish*) with which the rest of
the play is concerned.

Arden, in fact, is not greatly interested in economic man. Although a
theft of money is Butterthwaite's downfall, he scatters it cheerfully
about the stage, and the grasping, petty-minded quest for financial
favours which genuine corruption reveals whenever it is exposed in local
politics is far too trivial a theme for Arden. He relishes intrigue and
political manipulation for their own sake, as an exercise of the human intelligence, and the various machinations and counter-machinations in
The Workhouse Donkey have a slightly unreal air because of this fact:
although the play has a contemporary setting, it takes place in a land of
Arden's own invention, and *Armstrong's Last Goodnight*, where the
playwright's historical imagination gives him licence to create a whole
society on his own terms (and an expressive language to go with it) is a
more successful play on that account.

Armstrong's Last Goodnight has a large cast and is infrequently
revived; it is certainly not an easy play for most audiences. The plot is
complicated and, even when one has unravelled it, it is hard to see what
moral, if any, Arden wants us to draw from the action. The language, an
imaginative and flexible pastiche of sixteenth-century Lowlands Scots,
has its delights for the reader but requires an attentive ear, to say the
least, if its full value is to be extracted from a stage performance. But it
repays close attention, partly because it is the most subtle and satisfying
of Arden's earlier, 'uncommitted' works, and partly because, despite the
underlying gravity of its theme, its deft analysis of human motives is
enjoyable and zestfully sharp-witted.

Subtitled 'An Exercise in Diplomacy', it investigates the role of
deviousness in pursuit of a valid political aim. Whereas both *Serjeant
Musgrave's Dance* and *The Workhouse Donkey* contain central
characters whose inflexibility brings about their downfall, *Armstrong's
Last Goodnight* has the opposite—a schemer who casts aside all
protocol in furtherance of his aims. Typically enough, Arden introduces

this theme with a fine image of the contrast between the naked man and the social role implied by his costume. Entering upon his delicate mission, Sir David Lindsay first removes his 'splendid and delightful' herald's tabard:

> The rags and robes that we do wear
> Express the function of our life
> But the bawdy body that we bear
> Beneath them carries nocht
> But shame and greed and strife . . .
>
> Yet here I stand and maun contrive
> With this sole body and the brain within him
> To set myself upon ane man alive
> And turn his purposes and utterly win him.
> That coat is irrelevant:
> I will wear it nae further
> Till Armstrong be brocht
> Intill the King's peace and order.   (pp. 26–27)

Lindsay's antagonist Armstrong, the marauding border chieftain whose freebooting ways are inconvenient to the maintenance of the fragile peace between England and Scotland, clearly engages Arden's sympathies as much as Lindsay himself. On the one side stands the outsize figure whose lawless ways cannot be contained inside the restrictions of advancing civilization; on the other is the skilful diplomatist who pits his intelligence against superior strength. By matching the two against each other, and in characteristic fashion refusing to endow either with a monopoly either of virtue or of human frailty, Arden allows himself full scope for his exploration of political man in action.

The theme is integrated happily with Arden's feeling for language: the prose is supple, exact and full of irony; the verse draws imaginatively on the ballad tradition, and the transition from one to the other does not involve a violent change of idiom.

The pattern of *Serjeant Musgrave's Dance*, as we saw, included a series of acts of violence which highlighted Musgrave's demonstration in the town square and complicated the issues surrounding his protest against war. In *Armstrong's Last Goodnight*, too, the diplomatic manoeuvring is set within a recurrent pattern of violence and deceit. It begins in Act I scene 3, when Armstrong is first introduced to the audience and is seen celebrating a solemn reconciliation with his ancient rival Wamphray. However, Wamphray is guilty of the seduction of Meg Eliot, a kinsman through marriage of Armstrong, and he scornfully rejects the proposal that he should make amends by marrying the girl. Thus Wamphray seals his own fate: within a few minutes, lulled into a drunken stupor, he has been disarmed and is viciously murdered.

Johnny Armstrong's code of honour, then, is not without its blemishes, and the presence of Meg, half-crazed and crying out for vengeance, reminds us of his broken word of honour[24]. And his behaviour towards Wamphray echoes almost precisely the treatment meted out to him in the final scenes when, flattered by the King's promise of a 'fraternal welcome' while he travels the border country, he is tricked into surrendering his arms, overpowered and hung without ceremony.

Lindsay is a party to this deception; indeed it is he who delivers the invitation which dupes Armstrong. So the play turns full circle, and ends with Lindsay and Armstrong both implicated in a treacherous murder. It is significant that when Lindsay delivers the fatal invitation to Armstrong he wears his herald's tabard once more. His attempt to deal with Armstrong 'as ane man against ane man' has proved a failure:

> Alas, and mortal vanity,
> We are but back whaur we began.
> A like coat had on the Greekish Emperour
> When he rase up his brand like a butcher's cleaver:
> There was the knot and he did cut it.
> And deed of gravity. Wha daur dispute it? (p. 112)

Throughout the play, in fact, we see Lindsay's unofficial attempts to guide destiny running into one difficulty after another. First he offers a free pardon and an official title from the King to Armstrong, in return for the abandonment of his border raids: but Maxwell, Wamphray's protector, has the ear of the King, and delays in procuring the proffered office ensue. The attraction of his old ways is too strong for Armstrong: chafing at the delay he resumes his raids, encouraged by a Lutheran Evangelist under whose spell he has fallen.

Enthusiastically Lindsay extends the scope of his secret diplomacy, even floating a scheme to establish a kind of independent border state contained between Scotland and England—all, needless to say, without official backing, and his plans come to nothing. Before the end his devious entanglements have led to the death of his friend and secretary McGlass, stabbed and mortally wounded in a brush with the Evangelist. It is McGlass himself who points the moral for Lindsay:

> Ye did tak pride in your recognition of the fallibility of man. Recognize your ain, then, Lindsay: ye have ane certain weakness, ye can never accept the gravity of ane other man's violence. For you yourself hae never been grave in the hale of your life! (p. 108)

Lindsay's lack of 'gravity', his circuitous attempts to find a peaceful solution to affairs by relying on his own psychological prowess, eventually founder and are replaced by political butchery. What, then, is Arden's own moral stance in this sequence of events? Albert Hunt in his recent study of the dramatist maintains that Arden has, from the beginning of his career, been a 'revolutionary' dramatist[25]. It is certainly useful to be reminded that Arden is hardly the colourless liberal that some critics would make of him, but I am not sure that 'revolutionary' is a useful adjective to apply to the early Arden. All three of the plays we have been considering end with some kind of success for the established order of things, although we may note a progressive darkening of the image. The colliery town is well rid of Black Jack Musgrave, although Walsh's comment, delivered 'with great bitterness', reminds us that the world is not restored to perfect healthy thereby:

> The community's been saved. Peace and prosperity rules, We're all friends and neighbours for the rest of today. We're all sorted out. We're back where we were. So what do we do? (p. 99)

Equally the departure of Feng is a matter for rejoicing, counterbalanced by the rejection of Butterthwaite as a sort of scapegoat for the hypocrisy with which the community is loaded. In these two plays the banishment of the unyielding followers of 'straight lines' is clearly in accordance with Arden's general philosophy: what is interesting about *Armstrong's Last Goodnight* is that Lindsay's 'circuits' prove equally ineffectual. His reply to the young King's expression of satisfaction is sombre:

> The man is deid, there will be nae war with England: this year. There will be but small turbulence upon the Border: this year. And what we hae done is no likely to be forgotten: this year, the neist year, and mony year after that. Sire, you are King of Scotland.
>
> (p. 121)

Arden's view of society in these three plays, it seems to me, is not only complex but somewhat ambiguous as well. In the first two plays we end with a vision of social order that is a long way from the kind of cosmic harmony that some critics profess to find established in Shakespearian or Greek tragedy. The colliery town may be free of Black Jack Musgrave; but the heritage of violence and suppression that is instanced by the colonial war and the colliery lockout is inextricably a part of the fabric of that society; in *The Workhouse Donkey* Feng's departure is a recognition that unblemished incorruptibility is an impossible ideal for public life, but equally the fact that there is no room for Charlie Butterthwaite makes it clear that the final *status quo* is far from perfect. In *Armstrong's Last Goodnight* Arden quite evidently regards the maintenance of peace between the English and Scottish nations as a desirable and worthy objective, but shows that it cannot be achieved without an act of brutal treachery. The Arden who wrote these plays might be called a realist rather than a revolutionary, recognizing the necessary imperfections of society at the same time as he forces us to re-evaluate the moral issues that crop up within it. But above all both *Serjeant Musgrave's Dance* and *Armstrong's Last Goodnight* show a detestation of violence, and demonstrate one act of violence breeding further acts of the same nature. For the revolutionary, on the other hand, violence is seen as a necessary and inevitable preliminary to social change. In *The Bagman* we have seen how Arden expressed his doubts about the role of the dramatist as an impartial, if not impassive, observer; in the plays that have followed *The Bagman* there is, it seems to me, a marked development towards a more truly revolutionary view of the world.

The Island of the Mighty, in terms of sheer length, is the Ardens' most ambitious work. Their earlier drama is peppered with references to Arthurian legend, and in fact the central theme of the trilogy is something that had preoccupied Arden throughout his working life as a dramatist[26]. Successive versions (the first written as early as 1953) never saw the light of day, until the trilogy in its present form (with Margaretta D'Arcy collaborating on the final draft) was accepted for production by the Royal Shakespeare Company, who presented it (in December 1972) in the unhappy circumstances already related.

In every society there are some subjects which remain as a sort of standing challenge to the literary artist; and for the British the

Arthurian legend has been one such. From time to time poets have contemplated, with varying degrees of determination, taking up the shadowy history of this indigenous hero and refashioning it as a patriotic epic work to rival Homer's treatment of the Trojan wars or Virgil's *Aeneid*; and Arden, with his antipathy towards both the Romans and the Anglo-Saxons who carried on the unimaginative work of imposing order and discipline upon the unruly tribes of Britain, might have been expected to see in this British king locked in a vain fight against the tide of history a suitable subject for a major work.

There is, I think, a further pointer to the ambitious nature of *The Island of the Mighty*. Since the publication of Sir James Frazer's *The Golden Bough* at the end of the last century one of the subjects of perennial fascination to scholars, artists and writers has been the Year-King whose strength is the magical health of the primitive tribe until he is replaced by a rival in ritual combat. The fact that Frazer's theories have been largely rejected by modern anthropologists has not diminished their attraction, and they are one of the starting-points in the modern interest in the origins of myth and ritual. The first two parts of *The Island of The Mighty* touch extensively upon this theme, finally revealing Arthur himself as no stranger to the ancient, primitive rites supposedly abandoned by the introduction of Christianity[27].

The Island of the Mighty, then, gets to grips with two themes, one central to the British literary tradition and the other an important strand of modern thought. Add to this that the poet Merlin was an all-important member of Arthur's retinue, which enables Arden's concern for the role of the poet to emerge as a third and equally important *leitmotiv*, and we can see that *The Island of the Mighty* is a big play in scope as well as size.

A trilogy set in the Celtic twilight of Arthurian Britain, against a background of poet-magicians and primitive rituals, sounds like a dangerous formula for misty romanticism of the worst sort. With his usual astringent but creative perversity, Arden avoids the obvious pitfalls. One of his objects is to contrast the legend that has survived with the likely reality out of which it grew. Even in his own lifetime Arthur is shown to have become a mythical figure. 'I have heard of the Battle of Badon Hill', says Balin in the first part:

> There were man-eating giants there destroyed by a famous hero called Arthur. He had to help him a red dragon breathing fire . . . But I did not know . . . that he had verily existed. (p. 38)

The Arthur whom Arden actually presents on the stage is a far cry from this superhuman warrior; but the grizzled authoritarian with his shrewd yet waning political insight and his close attention to administrative detail is a more credible figure than the Arthur of myth and legend.

Similarly, Arden refuses to be overawed by the heady material of ritual and divine kingship. The rites of the Pictish tribes where matriarchy still holds its sway and the temporary King is chosen in deadly combat form the background of the first two plays, but they are shown in a period where their efficacy is increasingly subject to doubt, particularly on the part of the curiously rationalist figure of the Pictish Queen's War-Leader. And Merlin is a poet stripped of romanticism: he bends his talents to his monarch's political aims, with ultimately disastrous consequences for himself. In short, Arden devotes his historical imagination, not to bolstering up a wistful picture of a vanished golden age, but towards the stern task of 'demystifying' and 'demythologizing' the events which gave rise to Arthurian legend.

In a programme note John Arden refers to the modern parallels that he finds in his subject-matter:

> National myths of this sort present a picture of a way of life remarkably similar to that which exists today in the 'Third World' ... Just as the energy of Britain in the sixth century was concentrated among the wild tribesmen of the hills and the crude English just stepped from their black ships, so the Third World contains—to our alarm and perhaps our ultimate salvation—the strongest urge for social change and the keenest courage in bringing it about[28].

The play, he declares, tries to indicate 'something of how the early history of Britain foreshadows twentieth-century turbulence'. Here the history of the trilogy's long germination becomes important, for Arden's commitment to the revolutionary values of the Third World was to a large extent a consequence of his visit to India, and the final version was completed by the Ardens on their return. Both the early, 'uncommitted' Arden and the later, more radical writer have had a hand in *The Island of the Mighty*, and the play veers from objectivity to partisanship in a way that is sometimes fruitful but occasionally confusing. At times Arden seems to be mainly interested in getting us to revise our view of Arthur, just as earlier his historical imagination had worked upon Herod and King John; at times he seems more concerned with reminding us of the sufferings of the common people as the conflicting forces advance and retreat across the ravaged countryside.

Because of the somewhat mixed nature of the play, it is difficult to come down on one side or the other in the controversy between the Ardens and the Royal Shakespeare Company. As Albert Hunt argues, the crucial question is the treatment of King Arthur 'against a background of peasant suffering and poverty':

> Without the background of the peasants, the play can be interpreted as telling the tragic story of a once great kind in decline. The emphasis will then be on the pathos of an ageing hero. But, set against the peasant background, Arthur becomes a ludicrous, posturing figure. He demands to be presented with irony[29].

I think Hunt is right; the trouble is that the structure of the play forces attention away from the peasants, who remain very much on the periphery of events, and on to Arthur; and the irony to which Hunt refers is not always obvious.

In fact King Arthur is not, it seems to me, one of Arden's more successful characters. He lacks the self-awareness of Arden's other political figures, and consequently any irony that is around tends to be of the tragic kind, inviting our pity for the old warrior as he vainly tries to stave off the defeat that we know to be inevitable. Furthermore, Arden seems to have found difficulty in devising a suitable linguistic style for his Arthur. He has successfully avoided mock-heroic dialogue, and that is something to be thankful for, but Arthur's language, although literate and articulate, is too often colourless and needlessly prosaic.

Perhaps, then, it might be more profitable to turn from questions of language and structure to the staging and presentation of *The Island of the Mighty*, for in this region, it seems to me, the trilogy is full of interest. Arden, of course, has never been a naturalistic dramatist; but he has more or less progressively moved away from realism in his settings. *Serjeant Musgrave's Dance* requires a variety of localities—Arden specifies in his introduction that 'only those pieces of architecture, furniture, and properties actually *used* in the action need be present' (they, he adds, should be 'thoroughly realistic'). In *The Workhouse Donkey* the locations in the stage directions are equally specific; but there is less emphasis on scenic realism. The play has a fluid structure with a succession of shortish scenes, uses direct address to the audience, and was adapted for open staging at the Chichester Festival Theatre. In *Armstrong's Last Goodnight* we find Arden making successful use of the medieval system of 'simultaneous mansions'. Permanently on view throughout the play's performance are three scenic units: to the right and left of the stage are structures representing the Palace of Holyrood and Armstrong's Castle, and at the rear is a tree which represents the forest background against which the pattern of treachery and sexual betrayal is played out (and on whose branches Armstrong meets eventual doom). The stage itself, in accordance with medieval tradition, is 'unlocalized': Lindsay's diplomatic journeying is signalled simply by his crossing from one mansion to the other, and the action spills out whenever necessary from the mansions into the central area.

What Arden has done in this sequence of plays is to throw progressive emphasis upon the figure of the actor. *Armstrong's Last Goodnight* is a play which uses very little scenery but a great deal of spectacle: the importance of the herald's tabard which Lindsay casts aside and then takes up again has already been referred to, and with great effect Arden contrives for Armstrong to bedeck himself in finery which he has plundered from his victims before he marches proudly to his fateful meeting with the King[30]. Likewise with the language: the actors' dialogue is extended by the use of verse and formal rhetoric, establishing the setting far more imaginatively than the best designer's use of realistic scenery could ever do. *Armstrong's Last Goodnight*, in short, goes well beyond some formal borrowing from the conventions of medieval drama to shift the emphasis for dramatic expression back where it belonged in the Elizabethan theatre—on the actor, his costume and a few significant properties, and the language that the dramatist has given him. In the *Island of The Mighty* the language may not always reach the high points of *Armstrong's Last Goodnight* but the visual aspects of the play carry on and develop the work of the earlier play.

The staging techniques of *The Island of The Mighty* are not taken from any one historical period: they are an amalgam deriving from everything the Ardens have learnt during a working career packed with exploration and discovery, and are even influenced by the Indian folkplays the Ardens saw on their Asian visit[31]. From the Victorian Theatre comes the idea of painted backcloths changed for each scene, but the comment in the Notes to the play that they are 'emblems' rather than realistic scenery[32] reminds us of Arden's debt to the Medieval tradition. They are there to suggest not so much geographical locality as the great social and historical issues upon which the play concentrates its attention—a

Camp, a Raid, Ruins, a Seascape[33].

If the stage settings project the great issues with which the trilogy is concerned, the action played out in front of them similarly carries a load of meaning for the attentive spectator. 'The whole play', say the production notes, 'should be accompanied by music', not only as a background to the songs and some of the spoken verse speeches, but also 'to provide a strong rhythm for important pieces of movement and physical action'[34]. The scenes of 'movement and physical action' turn out on inspection to be mostly fights and combats, and the Ardens' intention (only partially realized in the RSC production) seems to have been to give them a knockabout, pantomime quality, while at the same time their recurrence throughout the play should bear some resemblance to the highly formal climaxes of stylized movement in, for instance, the Japanese Noh Drama. As well as these patterns of action, emphasized by the music, the visual appearance of the actors and their properties, in particular of Arthur, is of great importance within the trilogy.

Arthur is an aging warrior swimming vainly against the tide of history, and his failing strength is reflected in his physical appearance. The image of the lame king, as Albert Hunt argues[35], is one of the most powerful in the play: it is also a many-sided image. It certainly reflects the hollow nature of Arthur's power-base, as he stumps about the stage delivering his commands; but together with the scar that disfigures his forehead, it also has a deeper significance which, as we shall see, emerges only towards the end of the second part of the trilogy. For the audience has yet to learn that he was not crippled in battle, but in far more sinister circumstances. Accompanying Arthur in all his public moments is his battle standard. It is, say the Notes, 'an important property':

> . . . a long pole with a three-dimensional model of a long-tailed red dragon on top, and a square banner hung from a cross-bar. The banner bears the symbol of the Chi-Rho. A skull with a gold circlet round its brows is nailed to the cross-bar.   (p. 25)

For the moment we shall simply note the three symbols—the Christian emblem, the red dragon and the skull—and wait for their significance to emerge as our discussion of the trilogy's main themes develops.

Part I, *Two Wild Young Noblemen*, is mainly concerned with Balin and Balan, twins who successively fall subject to the primitive rites of the Pictish tribe of cat-women. Part II, *'O the Cruel Winter . . .'*, deals with the last phase of Arthur's reign, ending with his final defeat in the battle of Camlann, when the English troops overrun the divided British army. But the action of these two parts is only a framework upon which to hang the great thematic issues which engage the Ardens' interests. The court poet Merlin, delighted to hear himself described as 'a sideways man'[36], hurries from one part of the country to another in pursuit of Arthur's political aims, developing once again the Ardens' continual interest in the social responsibilities of the poet. Interwoven with this strand of the plot is another exploration of the heritage bred by acts of gratuitous violence. As soon as we meet the two 'wild young noblemen' in the second scene of the trilogy we find them fighting; and when, a little later, Merlin intervenes to end another squabble between the two brothers, he gets rewarded for his pains by a blow from Balin. 'The person of a Chief Poet is as sacred as an Ambassador', he cries in protest[37]. The chain of violence set in motion by this apparently trivial incident runs through the whole trilogy, involving the death of Balin and Balan in fratricidal combat, Merlin's own guilt and subsequent madness when he strikes the sacred figure of his fellow-poet Taliesin, and ending only when Merlin himself is killed at the very end of the trilogy.

The privileges and responsibilities of the poet and the disruptive nature of arbitrary violence are familiar Arden themes; but *The Island of The Mighty*, like all of Arden's historical works, also has its own specific subject-matter, rooted in the period in which the play is set. In the first two parts of this trilogy, indeed, this subject matter lies so thick on the ground that it is difficult to disentangle all the strands. Arden's delight in portraying the interaction of opposing groups is spread panoramically over an immense canvas as Arthur negotiates with his kinsmen and other potential allies, struggles against rivalries within his own camp, and tries to cope with the unruly Picts. There is a kind of descending order of civilization with Arthur, who regards himself as a Roman and a Christian, at one extreme, and at the other the untamed Pictish tribes with their matriarchal heritage and their captive kings; set against all these are the brutal English invaders, whose menace is glimpsed only through the presence of a captured warrior. Cross-cutting these groups are the poet-negotiators who pass from camp to camp under the protection of their sacred office, an assortment of women—kinsmen, wives and mistresses of the kings and poets—who come into their own in the second part of the trilogy, and the unhappy peasants whose only desire is to till their fields and tend their herds.

In the first part of the trilogy, through the adventures of the twins Balin and Balan, the Ardens explore the waning world of the matriarchal Picts. Arthur's cousin Strathclyde is concerned with little else except his perennial feud against the Picts, while to Arthur, who sees himself as entrusted with the historic mission of preserving the values of Christian Rome against the pressing threat of the English invasion, they are, it seems, an untidy reminder of the past and little more; nevertheless he finds himself engaged in the feud when, in the middle of a delicate arbitration between the Picts and Strathclyde, the impatient Balin (who unlike his brother has decided to cast his lot with Arthur) strikes the Pictish ambassador dead. This important scene (the second half of Scene Three) is very characteristic of Arden. Arthur, the weak king, appears dressed for the occasion in the full splendour of a general of the Imperial Roman army: the fine and necessary balance between two opposing groups is almost established by his subtle skill in negotiating when, in a spectacular 'overstepping of the mark', Balin destroys it with a wild act of violence; and this murderous action is, of course, one link in the chain of violence which we have already mentioned, leading directly to his own death at the end of the first part.

The wandering Balan, in the meantime, has been captured by the Picts and chosen in the ordained manner as their new King. Without realizing what is happening he is led to the place of combat, Merlin describing the action as it is represented on the stage:

> They lead him out as drunk as a dog
> They set his feet into a boat

Across the dark water of their lake
Unto their little island he must float . . .   (p. 66)

His opponent, lamed so that he cannot escape and weakened by his
luxurious reign 'for a year and a day', is no match for him and Balan easily easily establishes himself as victor in mortal combat. Already the Pictish War-Leader has voiced his misgivings about the coming ritual. If
Balan's life is to be spared, he pleads, let him use it 'for the benefit of the
people':

> He is a fighter. Before all else, let him fight. In the place where he is
> most needed. Without doubt that is the battle against the soldiers
> of Strathclyde.   (p. 62)

And after his victory Balan, 'suddenly a little sobered', reflects on the victory over his opponent:

> Could he have once been a stranger like myself
> Who had to fight for his life here without any choice . . .?
> It is in my mind these people
> Have some customs that are not good.   (p. 67)

Arden, as we have already suggested, is taking a critical view of the
rites of this pagan society, and showing the historic moment of change
when this archaic piece of savagery no longer seems sufficient for the
needs of society. And in fact when Balin, fleeing from Arthur's court
after his disastrous intervention in the negotiations with Strathclyde, is
himself captured and set to combat with his own brother (who, in his
turn, is lamed and weakened by self-indulgence), the ceremony is performed for the last time. When the masks are removed the two brothers,
both mortally wounded, each discover who their opponent was. 'These
people have ill customs', are Balan's dying words, and the Pictish poet
glosses them:

> We make our King lame so that he cannot escape. And then after all
> his pleasuring the next King finds it easy to kill him. Until now the
> custom was good. But certain of our people came to believe that it
> should be put an end to, and I think that that is what the Goddess
> has now done.   (p. 98)

There are other themes in the first part of the trilogy, including an
extended scene with one Pellam, a half-crazed fanatic who disputes
Arthur's claim to be the leader of Christian Britain until he, too, is killed
by the wild Balin: but central to all the rest is the decline of the Pictish
custom of the maimed king. Part I, then, charts a process of historical
change; and so, too, does Part II: but the surprise which the second part
of the trilogy holds in store is that the change does not involve the sort
of progress towards a world of ever greater enlightenment which we
sometimes naively picture as the course of history, but rather a reversion
towards the customs and beliefs of pre-Christian, pre-Roman Britain.
Here it is perhaps helpful to remember the parallels which the Ardens
have drawn between the Britain of *The Island of the Mighty* and the
Third World of today. Arthur and Pellam are in a sense relics of a former
colonial civilization, reminiscent of the anglicized Indians and Africans,
with their memories of Sandhurst and Balliol, who were the immediate

75

successors to British Imperial power, while the younger Medraut represents the next generation of leaders, less affected by this alien scale of values. But in Arthur, too, it eventually becomes apparent that the Romano-Christian civilization which he proudly proclaims as his own (and to which Merlin eventually sacrifices his sanity) is something imposed upon a deeper residue of British culture.

If Part I of *The Island of the Mighty* shows the decline of a matriarchal society, Part II reverses the pattern and portrays the resurgence of an archaic matrilineal culture in the confusion of Arthur's declining hegemony. Even more than in the first part, the material of the drama is presented in a dual light, directly as well as obliquely through the moral perspective of the poets involved in the developing action.

We are introduced to a new poet, Aneurin, of a more revolutionary cast than Merlin or his venerable preceptor Taliesin. In the first scene Aneurin attends a concourse of the College of Bards, assembled to consider his claim to the title of Chief Poet. Required to submit an ode commemorating 'the Burial of the Head of Bran the Blessed, ancestor of all the royal houses of the Island of the Mighty', he shocks the gathering with his opening lines:

> I was a wicked man
> And I had a wicked wife
> I could not endure her
> To live her wicked life.
>
> I could not endure her
> Nor yet could I leave her
> Whatever she said to me
> I did not dare believe her   (p. 104)

The audience needs an alert and capacious mind to catch the full significance of this amusing scene: for it is some time before it becomes apparent that the rebellious Aneurin knows a great deal more than the bards who reject his poem about the heritage of Bran and Branwen, ancestors of the British people, and that the 'wicked wife' of his poem bears a strong resemblance to the claimant for the ancient matriarchal throne of Britain that we are to meet a little later.

The second scene switches from the Assembly of Bards to Arthur's camp; and now comes the first suggestion that Arthur himself is more interested in the history of Bran the Blessed than might have been suspected from his official bearing in the first part of the trilogy. In conversation with Merlin it is revealed that the skull fixed to the top of his battle-standard is none other than the skull of Bran, which was to have been the subject of Aneurin's composition; according to the legend, it would guard the safety of the British as long as it remained buried 'beneath its cairn of stones'. Merlin reminds Arthur how he said that he would nail the skull to his standard 'so that all your soldiers would know that a dead man is but dead: it takes a living man to lift him up'. Arthur had intended to 'make a great declaration' on the subject to his troops; but in the end it was kept secret from all except Merlin (although the Pictish Ambassador evidently knew something about it). In an important speech, Arthur explains his change of heart:

You see, *I* am aware that I have resisted superstition. Britain is not protected by the head of an ancient hero turned into a discredited god. It is protected by an experienced Army under orders of a careful and Christian General, who alone among his countrymen has read books full of good sense. Titus Livius, Julius Caesar—when I was young you could still lay hands on them and learn how to put them together, word upon word, chapter upon chapter. I cut my hair short, I turned myself back into a cool-headed Roman. But my Companions were not quite that: Bran the Blessed was their ancestor. It came to me suddenly that were I to deprive them of him I might well be letting leak the darkest blood of their courageous hearts. So in silence I put him up, as a message to myself alone.   (pp. 107–108)

Now the battle-standard is revealed as a kind of emblem of the stratification of British society: the Red Dragon (ensign of the Roman troops in Britain) and the Chi-Rho sign indicating the Romano-Christian heritage which Arthur is struggling to maintain, the grinning skull above bearing testimony to the half-forgotten but ever-present stamp of the ancient British culture. And psychologically Arthur himself reflects the same ambiguities: in his rational self he is a 'careful and Christian general', but his secret and defiant gesture in digging up the skull of Bran reveals another layer of his personality, and he is not quite free himself from a nagging fear of the old superstitions.

These opening scenes prepare the way for the later emergence of Gwenhwyvar, sister of the petty prince Gododdin, as the authentic 'daughter of Branwen', whose warrior-husband is to be the chosen leader of the British. The Ardens treat their material circuitously, reserving for the closing scenes the revelation that in his youth Arthur himself was chosen by a 'daughter of Branwen', and that his lieutenant Medraut, supposed by all to be his nephew, is in fact his own son by an incestuous union with his sister, the wife of Strathclyde:

Yes, my own sister had me creep into her bed, because Morgan told us it was needful—for the security of the land. The wife of Strathclyde was the Daughter of Branwen, you see—I was marked upon my head, I was made lame by a strange ceremony. (p. 168)

And so finally Arthur, the Roman General fighting under the banner of Christ, is revealed as no different from Balin and Balan, lamed and scarred according to the superstitious rites of the 'wicked wives' of pre-Roman Britain. By holding back this revelation a sense of mystery is created throughout the second part of the trilogy—at the expense, it might be argued, of clarity for the audience. Without this vital knowledge, we lose the full significance of the growing rivalry between the ageing Arthur and Medraut, intent on developing new military tactics and christening his troops 'the Hounds of Bran'. It obscures, too, the sinister nature of the marriage proposed by Gododdin between Arthur and his young widowed sister. Only in retrospect does it become clear why the marriage night between the two is symbolized by 'a very violent dance—a mime of battle rather than love-making'[38] for which the two have donned ferocious masks; the audience must wait until, a few scenes later, the aged Morgan, Arthur's crone-like sister, emerges from hiding to awaken Gwenhwyvar's memories of the 'games' she played as a girl which establish her as the secret successor in the line of the daughters of Branwen. For after the death of Bran, she explains:

> *Branwen* buried his head: and from then on—she and her daughters—they have lived in perpetual slavery. The one who is to be Queen is chosen at her birth, by those who are instructed. There are certain signs—not easy to be recognized. When the child is a little older there are certain things she must remember . . . (p. 150)

Eventually Gwenhwyvar places the mark of the scar upon Medraut's forehead, establishing him and not Arthur as her champion and consort. Masked and exultant, he is presented by Gwenhwyvar to the people, and cries:

> The Island of the Mighty belongs to us, it belongs to all of us, it belongs to the Children of Branwen—and we shall never let it go! (p. 164)

Now the conflict between Arthur and Medraut is inevitable, and it is this conflict, the battle of Camlann, which seals the fate of both sides and of Britain itself.

Another obscure feature of the second part of *The Island of the Mighty* is the role of Merlin, the 'sideways man' who acts as diplomat for Arthur. In his brief study of the trilogy, Albert Hunt notes his affinity to Lindsay in *Armstrong's Last Goodnight*:

> He is urbane, intelligent, clever, well-intentioned, self-critical. But he has allowed himself to be used by what he calls 'the wolf-pack'—King Arthur and his army. And when he is finally called on to act, he fails, and goes on to retreat into his private madness . . .[39]

But there is an element of sincerity and dedication in Merlin's actions which Hunt perhaps overlooks. One of the first to become aware of the danger Medraut will pose to Arthur, he declares in a soliloquy:

> I none the less must set my mind to hold this blind and ignorant general
> Erect and tall against the ebbtide and the flood—
> if he should fall
> Five hundred years of history will all be overwhelmed
> Swilled away to nowhere in a pagan bog of blood and mud . . .
> (p. 141)

And so when Taliesin, declaring that 'the highest function of our traditional craft is the mediation of peace'[40], attempts to heal the breach between the two on the eve of the fatal battle, Merlin—ignoring the sanctity of the poet-ambassador—attacks him violently and nearly kills him. It is this action, continuing the pattern of violence initiated by Balin at the beginning of the first part, and symbolizing Merlin's self-destruction as a poet, which drives him into the world of insanity. 'Merlin is a bird!' he cries as the closing words of the second part. 'Merlin grows feathers! Merlin will fly everywhere . . .'

Once again, the Ardens have refused to endow either side of a conflict with a monopoly of virtue. The Romano-Christian ideals of Arthur's tattered imperialism have their inadequacies exposed, but the thoughtless savagery of the tribal world-view, represented by the Picts in the first part and by Gwenhwyvar, Morgan and Medraut in the second, is equally insufficient for the needs of a floundering 'post-colonial' nation. And the poets—Taliesin, vainly trying to reconcile the two opposing sides, Merlin, suicidally casting his lot with what he conceives as 'five hundred years of history', even Aneurin, with his knowledge of the 'wicked wives' and his intuitive understanding of 'the cruel winter, and the pain of its arrival'—are helpless in the face of the ignorance of their political leaders. The tragic result of these weaknesses and divisions in British society is the battle of Camlann, which opens the way for the English invaders; the consequences, reflected at the political level by the suffering and oppression of the common people, and at the imaginative level by Merlin's madness, form the material for the third part of the trilogy.

Arthur, Medraut, Strathclyde and the other princes are now dead; Bedwyr, Arthur's dour standard-bearer, and a handful of war-weary companions are all that is left of the once mighty British army. Bedwyr's lack of an adequate sense of direction as he tries to hold the army together is reflected by his lack of a poet-politician to guide his counsels and his attempts to capture and restore to health the unfortunate Merlin. Before the end of the play he has abandoned his military responsibilities, symbolically hurling the famous Arthurian sword into a lake and retreating to the solitude of an isolated religious community.

The demented Merlin hovers on the outskirts of the action (his official costume as chief poet replaced by a masked outfit symbolizing his madness), a reminder of the confusion and divided loyalties which reached their climax in his attack upon Taliesin. Merlin is the only character to play an important role in all three parts of the trilogy; but whereas the first two parts presented him against a background of political and military manoeuvring, in the third part the setting is the ravaged and depopulated countryside of the Britain that had fallen an easy prey to the English invaders. The history of Merlin's madness and his eventual restoration to sanity is to a large extent the story of an unconscious search for a new role for the poet, free from the compromises and betrayals inherent in Merlin's former role.

Only at the end of the play is he coaxed back to human companionship when the saintly Bedwyr persuades a cowman's wife to leave him food each night. At length Merlin's poetic inspiration, dulled and eventually destroyed in the service of Arthur, returns as he addresses the cowman's wife:

> By God but I will make a verse about the way your mouth turns up
> —[*He sings*]
> It came so quick it came so warm
> Across your face of fear
> As a man might see on a frozen moor
> The running of the wild red deer—! (p. 233)

A moment later the cowman, spying Merlin with his wife and suspecting the worst, springs upon him and kills him in the final act of violence which rounds off the trilogy.

The Ardens declare that the main theme of *The Island of the Mighty* is 'the relationship of the poet to society', and the final moment of this theme is Merlin's cure, and the return of his poetic inspiration, as a result of the simple, good-hearted actions of the cowman's wife—a far cry from the intrigue and power-politics which formed the staple diet of Merlin and the other chief poets in the first two parts of the trilogy. It is left to Aneurin, the poet who has never fully submitted to the conventions of officialdom, to drive home the message:

> The poet without the people is nothing. The people without the poet will still be the people . . . All that we can do is to make loud and to make clear their own proper voice. They have so much to say . . .   (p. 232)

So far as the Ardens' own development is concerned, this conception of the poet as the 'proper voice' of the people is probably the most important of the many themes to emerge from *The Island of the Mighty*. *The Ballygombeen Bequest* was first staged (in Belfast—no-one can accuse the Ardens of believing that discretion is the better part of valour) in May 1972, some six months before *The Island of the Mighty*, but it is appropriate to conclude this chapter by discussing it since it is, as Albert Hunt says, 'the first of the Ardens' plays to take up a clear-cut Marxist position'[41]. Whereas in the massive (and sometimes cumbersome) *Island of the Mighty* the voice of the dispossessed is often muffled as the dramatists pursue their manifold interests across the length and breadth of ancient Britain, in *The Ballygombeen Bequest* it rings out with a concentrated conviction that marks it off from the Ardens' earlier work: the Ardens have harnessed their talents to the people, 'to make loud and to make clear their own proper voice'.

As Brecht knew, taking up a Marxist position is not simply a question of expressing emotional sympathy with the victims of capitalism; with its emphasis on destroying the dominant 'ideology' of bourgeois society, Marxism requires its dramatists to build a clear understanding of the social and economic framework of society into their plays. The task is not an easy one: indeed, there are so many question marks attached to orthodox Marxist doctrine that compromises of artistic integrity are often necessary. Human experience and the party line often point in different directions; what makes *The Ballygombeen Bequest* stand out among political plays is the way in which the two are welded together with subtlety and feeling. It seems a simple, even a slight play, but in fact it marks the point at which most of the problems troubling John Arden when he wrote *The Bagman* find their resolution.

The Ballygombeen Bequest bears the hallmarks of a later Arden play. It is, says the introductory stage direction, 'intended for as fluid a presentation as possible': the stage settings are reduced to a minimum, and the action is accompanied by music. Unlike *The Island of the Mighty*, which calls for the resources of a major theatre company, *The Ballygombeen Bequest* can be performed by a cast of seven—with the result that in its first professional production the small, dedicated group of young actors in the 7:84 Company was able to achieve what the mighty Royal Shakespeare Company had failed to achieve with the trilogy, and created a form of 'rough theatre' completely adapted to the needs of the play. But although, as we have said, *The Ballygombeen Bequest* marks a new departure for the Ardens, it also looks back to many of the distinctive features we discovered in the early Arden plays.

The participants in the action are divided into two groups, each defined by their social role. On one side is the family of Irish tenants, on the other the English estate agent who exploits them, aided and abetted by his devious lawyer Crotchet and, in the latter half of the play, by the 'forces of law and order' as represented by the British troops in Northern Ireland. The sympathies of the Ardens naturally favour the Irish peasants rather than their English landlord, but now the Arden's long-standing distaste for the Anglo-Saxon world-view takes on harsh political overtones, as the absentee landlord Hollidey-Cheype gradually emerges in his true colours as a type of capitalist oppression throughout the world. (And it should be noted that the villainous Hagan, an Irish contractor on the make, is every bit as bad as Hollidey-Cheype, with the additional crime of proving a traitor to his own countrymen.) In *The Ballygombeen Bequest* the 'overstepping of the mark' which served to upset the balance between the two groups in the earlier plays is, so to speak, built into the characters of Holliday-Cheype and Hagan in their role as exploiters of the poor; nevertheless the play reaches its climax with a vicious act of violence for which Holliday-Cheype, Hagan, and the British and Irish security forces must all accept a share of the responsibility.

The action of the play begins in the post-war jubilation of 1945, and ends among the harsh divisions of the contemporary world in 1972. The history of Hollidey-Cheype's exploitation of his Irish 'tenants' over two generations mirrors Anglo-Irish relations over the same period, and by extension the widening gap between rich and poor in the postwar world at large. Obviously this historical perspective gives an added complexity to the dramatic conflict between Hollidey-Cheype and the O'Leary family, but—in marked contrast to *The Island of the Mighty*— it is all presented with the utmost clarity and economy of detail. Structurally, the sense of political change is represented by the difference between Seamus O'Leary and his son Padraic, who replaces him as head of the household half-way through the play; and in a few deft strokes the language of the Narrator enlarges this contrast into a picture of the poor and oppressed in the world of today.

In fact in the language of *The Ballygombeen Bequest* the Ardens hit upon the most successful and unified style since *Armstrong's Last Goodnight*. Whenever John Arden can draw upon a popular vernacular tradition his language—verse and prose alike—always receives a boost, and here the language of the Irish peasantry, with its closeness to a genuine tradition of balladry, provides a stimulating source of imagery (which the dramatists draw upon, it might be added, without descending to the stock verbal routines of stage Irishry); but as well as the simple, dignified speech of the harassed Irish peasants there is the polished, ironical self-awareness of Hollidey-Cheype and his accomplice Crotchet and the bitter energy of the Narrator's verse.

In *The Ballygombeen Bequest* most of the action involves the property which Holliday-Cheype unexpectedly inherits from a distant relative; and just as Holliday-Cheype himself and his Irish dependants come to be representatives of the two sides of the class struggle, so too the profitable holiday home and the tumbledown cottage alongside, in which the O'Learys have lived rent-free for generations, stand as symbols of the economic relationship between them. The property, its plumbing, the state of the O'Learys' roof, the legal entanglements surrounding it, are all presented in vivid detail, and one of the major achievements of the play is the way in which all these minute particulars (not visibly on the stage of course, but everpresent in the words and action) express the wider context. The difficult task, which confronts most artists with ideas to communicate, of making the link between the particular and the general is something at which Arden has not always been wholly successful in the past. In *Armstrong's Last Goodnight* and *The Island of the Mighty*, for instance, it requires quite an effort on the part of the audience to make the imaginative leap from sixteenth-century Scotland or fifth-century Britain to the general political principles the action is intended to illustrate; in *The Ballygombeen Bequest* everything is clearcut and unambiguous. This is partly, of course, because the doctrine of Marxism leaves no room for the delicate moral balancing acts in which the earlier Arden delighted, but it also represents a genuine artistic advance.

In the opening scene the bitter struggle that is to come is only hinted at, with Hollidey-Cheype venturing upon an occasional 'Begorrah' as he inspects his new property, while the O'Learys fill their required role as picturesque retainers. For Hollidey-Cheype, returning to civilian life after his none-too-rigorous war service, the chief attraction of his Irish estate is that it is free from the clutches of 'comrade Attlee's new government'. 'No rationing over there', his solicitor tells him, 'you can buy a ham in the West of Ireland the size of a bishop's buttock' [42]. Moving forward to 1956, the second scene begins to expose Hollidey-Cheype in his true colours. The narrator places the action in its historical setting:

> Eleven years for good or ill
> The Age of Austerity is over the hill.
> The Tories are in and Labour is out—
> Private Enterprise runs about
> On all four feet like a wolf in the night . . .   (p. 13)

Hollidey-Cheype, announcing an appointment with 'a certain Mr Rachman of Notting Hill Gate', is expanding his interests. The rising tide of prosperity—'export, import, cash, and credit'—he confidently asserts, has put an end even to the Irish question:

> The roaring hope of bomb and burst and blood at last is muted—
> King Billy and the Pope now both inhabit
> The yielding mattress of your Wall Street whore—   (p. 16)

But the new affluence of the fifties, as the Narrator reminds the audience, is far from universal:

> The figures of unemployment throughout Ireland
> Increase and increase
> The emigrant ships across the Irish Sea
> Heave seasick onwards and do not cease.   (p. 17)

The growing divisions in the wider world are mirrored in a new tension that creeps into the relationship between Hollidey-Cheype and his Irish dependants. Despite his growing wealth, the land-owner is unwilling to make improvements to the rapidly deteriorating condition of the

O'Learys' cottage, and is angered when they set the work in train themselves. One of the most important scenes in the play arises out of this action, and it might well be described as a miniature model for political drama. Crotchet has advised Hollidey-Cheype that the O'Learys will be entitled to claim 'squatters' rights' and assume legal ownership of their cottage unless he acts fast by replacing the old unwritten agreement between the two parties with a carefully worded and signed contract.

Crossing over to Ireland, Hollidey-Cheype confronts O'Leary with the unauthorized improvements to his cottage. Seamus begins by replying with bold but dignified defiance:

> 'Tis the same tale we have been told in Connacht for three hundred years: the poor man's roof is worth nothing till he makes it worth something, and every particle of that worth is directly diverted to the strongbox of the landlord. And what benefit has the landlord put into the land—by construction, by muscular toil, by the hump of his shoulders or the blistering of his skin?... I tell you truth, me bold Colonel: O'Leary is not deceived—nor will he be intimidated. (p. 23)

Hollidey-Cheype responds by exploiting Seamus' weakness, the old Irish frailty of drunkenness. Feigning a reasonable attitude while he plies Seamus with whiskey, he produces the legal document for the Irishman to sign; naturally he hurries over the fatal clause which, in ten years' time, is to give him the right under the law to evict the O'Learys from the house they have occupied for over a century.

Within the space of a few minutes Seamus' attitude has changed from proud and defiant patriotism to craven servility and, repeating 'Thank you, sir, you're very good', he ignorantly signs away his rights. Hollidey-Cheype's victory is an easy one: in the face of opposition from such as Seamus, he and his like have little to fear, and everything in this scene, from the pocket-flask which Hollidey-Cheype produces at the opportune moment to the legal jargon with which he confuses Seamus, points a political lesson in the mechanics of exploitation.

This scene forms the climax of the first part of the play, and is followed by another leap forward in time:

> From nineteen-fifty-seven
> To nineteen-sixty-eight
> The fat men of the fat-half world
> Had food on every plate.
> The lean men of the naked world
> Grew leaner every day ... (p. 25)

At the level of the O'Learys' family life the new intensity of the struggle between rich and poor is reflected in the figure of Padraic, Seamus' son, whose political education has taken place on a Manchester building site. The Irish Labour Party, he tells his family

> ... have yet to learn what I have learned and what you can not have learned at that convent school of yours. I mean the Concept of Mass Support and the Solidarity of the Working Class! (p. 29)

Padraic's political awareness is still brash and overconfident, but now that his family faces the threat of eviction after his father's death, his opposition poses a realistic threat to Hollidey-Cheype that Seamus, in his drunkenness and ignorance, could never have managed.

But it is not only Hollidey-Cheype who is menaced by Padraic: for the Ardens the exploitation of a country like Ireland is not simply the responsibility of absentee landlords. Within Ireland itself the selfish greed of capitalism is at work, and in *The Ballygombeen Bequest* it is represented by the sinister figure of Hagan, whose rise to power is skilfully charted by the dramatists. We first come across him as the owner of the local petrol pump, with an inside knowledge of all the village gossip; it is he who is responsible for the unauthorized alterations to the O'Leary cottage[43]. By the time that Padraic returns from England he has a sharp financial interest in the tourist and property industry that is despoiling Ballygombeen, and Padraic's brand of fiery socialism is something that he determines to destroy.

Two further powers unite to deal with the threat of Padraic's agitation—the security forces of England and Ireland. Arden's fondness for a display of intrigue in action shapes the closing scenes of the play, but here the intellectual enjoyment of the mechanics of the plot gives way to a harsh and merciless display of the depths to which political man will lower himself to suppress his enemies. Returning from a journey across the border to Northern Ireland, Padraic is stopped by British paratroops and dies in the course of a particularly brutal 'interrogation in depth'. The chain of events leading up to this climax is complicated, involving as it does the British and Irish security forces with their minions in murky alliance, Hollidey-Cheype himself, who invokes his wartime contacts to alert the British Secret Service to the threat from Ballygombeen, and the vicious Hagan, who plays a key role in getting the Dublin Special Branch involved[44].

The message is clear—or rather, it ought to be, for some critics interpreted the play as being violently and irrationally biased against the British role in Northern Ireland. To the Ardens the troubles in Ulster are an extension of the class struggle disguised as a sectarian dispute, and the freedom of North and South alike are shackled by 'the Man with the Long Purse'[45]. Once this is realized by Padraic and his like an alliance between the Irish and English forces of repression and their masters and collaborators, the exploiting capitalists of both lands, becomes inevitable; and this, rather than any simple condemnation of the behaviour of British troops, is the lesson taught by Padraic's downfall. Whereas a simple piece of legalistic trickery was enough to deal with his father, Padraic's political education threatens the whole established system.

But, behind the overt political scheme of the play, I think we may discern Arden's old distaste for the forces of law and order, crushing but never completely eliminating the quick and zestful Celtic appetite for life, a point which the final scene will emphasize.

The normal state of capitalism is ruthless competition rather than friendly co-operation and, Padraic once disposed of, Hagan and Hollidey-Cheype emerge as rivals once more. Hagan has already given a helping hand to the IRA when they took it upon themselves to bomb Hollidey-Cheype's bungalow, revealing the sordid self-interest behind his action in direct address to the audience:

He is going to have to sell it—
But once the lads have got their mark on it
What purchaser will dare
To put in a bid for that accursed piece of land—
Except of course a patriotic man
Who can prove his good intention
By the brave work of his own hand? (p. 41)

Taking the hint, the worsted Hollidey-Cheype finally abandons his Irish
interests altogether. 'The main chance is now in Europe', he declares[46].

In the final scene the Ardens point the moral of their tale; and to do so,
they turn not to a summing-up from the narrator, but to one of the oldest
and simplest of theatrical forms, knockabout farce. Shortly after
Padraic's funeral Hollidey-Cheype arrives in Ireland clutching a paper:

A most horrifying letter from Timothy Hagan! My bungalow has
been blown up! And he has the nerve to offer me what he calls a fair
price for the site! (p. 48)

The squabble between the two moneygrabbers deteriorates into
slapstick, with the two hurling pies taken from Padraic's funeral meal at
each other while they fight like children for possession of a pile of
banknotes. Padraic, of course, is dead; but his ghost haunts this final
scene. Rising from his bier, his face whitened, he sings softly:

They have killed me dead and laid me down
They have covered me up and buried me under
The men of power and pride confide
I can never arise and blow them asunder—
    Giddy-i-aye liddi-i-eye
  Giddy-i-aye I am dead for certain
    Giddi-i-aye tiddle-iddle-oo
    How many more like me? (p. 48)

It is Padraic who stirs up the trouble between Hagan and Hollidey-
Cheype, delivering covert blows to each of them which they assume to
come from their opponent, and when Hollidey-Cheype announces his intention of quitting Ireland for good, it is he who has the last word:

When you act in a play it is easy to say
That we shall win and never be defeated
When you go from here it is not so clear
That power for the people is predestined—
    Giddy-i-aye but don't forget . . .
    There are more of us than them . . . (p. 50)

For the moment, then, while the O'Leary family's troubles are undiminished, Hagan and Hollidey-Cheype remain in control of their fortunes; but their time is limited. The *reductio ad absurdum* of their activities to a childish battle over a wad of banknotes is one way of indicating this, and another, looking beyond the confined horizon of the
play itself, is the last message of Padraic's ghost.

The final image which *The Ballygombeen Bequest* leaves with the
spectator—and, at the time of writing, the final image which the Ardens
leave with us—is of capitalism doomed and tottering, its criminality

reduced to the proportions of lunatic farce. It is a far cry from the subtle ambivalence of the earlier Arden, but at the same time it is a logical progression from it (if 'logical' is ever the right word to apply to an artist's development). For the Ardens have always combined a fascination with the workings of society with a fierce love of freedom. For other dramatists, the personal experience which life inevitably carries in its train may lead to a new appraisal of human personality and a greater depth and compassion in its presentation, but for the Ardens it is the social framework and its relationship with personal freedom that have been glimpsed with a new awareness. If this sounds an empty phrase—particularly to those who regard Marxism as a damper upon creativity and artistic independence—the vigour, precision and artistry of *The Ballygombeen Bequest* stand not only as a vindication of the Ardens' altered political viewpoint, but also as a proof that their ceaseless experimentation and search for new forms of theatrical expression has proved splendidly fruitful.

Notes to Chapter 3

1 Arden himself has acknowledged the debt in his article 'An Embarrassment to the Tidy Mind', *Gambit* VI. 22(1972), pp. 30–36
2 *Sunday Times*, November 8, 1959
3 For a descriptive review of this piece, see Simon Trussler 'Political Progress of a Paralyzed Liberal', *TDR/The Drama Review* XIII. 4(T44), 1969, pp. 181–191
4 pp. xi–xii
5 *Two Autobiographical Plays*, p. 10
6 *Ibid.*, p. 17
7 Letter to *The Guardian*, 5 December 1972
8 *The Island of the Mighty*, p. 100
9 'Telling a True Tale' in *The Encore Reader*, p. 127
10 *Three Plays*, Penguin Books, 1964
11 p. 14
12 pp. 8–9
13 *The Empty Space* (London, 1968), p. 65
14 p. 17
15 pp. 84–85
16 *New Statesman*, 24 October 1959
17 *Daily Express*, 23 October 1959
18 *John Arden*, pp. 21–22
19 p. 64
20 p. 98
21 pp. 17, 55, 71, 93, 97
22 pp. 37, 52
23 *John Arden*, pp. 44–46
24 Eg pp. 105ff.
25 *Arden: A Study of his Plays* (London, 1974), p. 21
26 See the 'Author's Preface (1)' to the published edition
27 Arden's direct source for this strand of the plot was 'Robert Graves's intricate, enormous, and (to me at that time) extremely disorientating book *The White Goddess*, (pp. 10–11)
28 'The Matter of Britain', in *Flourish* 1972/73, Issue 3
29 *Arden*, pp. 158–159
30 pp. 144ff
31 p. 20
32 p. 23
33 pp. 23–24
34 p. 25
35 *Arden*, p. 159

36 p. 57
37 p. 42
38 p. 127
39 *Arden*, p. 160
40 p. 169
41 *Arden*, p. 153
42 p. 7
43 pp. 9, 17
44 p. 41
45 p. 28
46 p. 49

4 Harold Pinter: journey to the interior

Since the preceding Chapter began with a quotation revealing what I believe to be one of Harold Hobson's blind spots, it is only fair to begin this one by pointing out that Hobson was alone among the London reviewers in recognizing the merits of *The Birthday Party*. The first-night critics had all taken the view that *The Birthday Party* was (to quote W A Darlington) 'one of those plays in which an author wallows in symbols and revels in obscurity'[1]. It was Hobson who understood that the crucial point about *The Birthday Party* was that *there were no symbols* to be interpreted:

> The fact that no-one can say precisely what it is about, or give the address from which the intruding Goldberg and McCann come, or say precisely why it is that Stanley is so frightened by them is, of course, one of its greatest merits[2].

Harold Hobson's Sunday review came too late to save the play, which had closed the previous night. It was hardly a promising beginning for a writer with only a handful of published poems and a one-act play to his credit. But by 1960, when *The Room* received its first professional performance, along with *The Dumb Waiter*, at the Hampstead Theatre Club, Hobson observed with justifiable satisfaction that there was 'not a jutting frieze, buttress, nor coign of vantage but has its spectator'[3].

1960 was, in fact, an *annus mirabilis* for Pinter. In March, ITV broadcast *The Birthday Party* and 'for days', asserts Martin Esslin, 'one could hear people in buses and canteens eagerly discussing the play as a maddening but deeply disturbing experience'[4]. April saw the opening of *The Caretaker* at the Arts Theatre Club, from where it transferred to the West End for a highly successful run. There were performances of his radio and television plays, and he began to attract notice in Europe and the USA.

Since 1960 Pinter's output has been far from prolific. There have been three full-length stage plays and the theatrical double bill *Landscape* and *Silence*. These are backed up by a number of radio and television plays, many of which have also been presented in stage versions, a handful of revue sketches which some critics treat with almost as much reverence as the major plays, and the much-acclaimed adaptations for the screen of novels by writers as diverse as L P Hartley and Penelope Mortimer.

For many writers a rapid elevation to fame and favour is followed by a more depressing return journey as critics reach the conclusion that their former superlatives were a little excessive, or else judge that the promise of early days has not been matched by later achievement. With Pinter the situation is rather different. Harold Hobson, of course, is no longer alone among reviewers in singing the praises of each new play, but it soon becomes clear that for every Pinter enthusiast there is someone else who remains impervious to his charms. Simon Trussler points out that Pinter's plays are often more easy to assess at a second sitting, when the startling unexpectedness of plot and structure has worn off a little[5]; but there are many people, knowledgeable critics among them, who cannot be won over to a Pinter play however often they have seen it. The problem is that the critical division extends even to those admirers who have pondered the plays more deeply and been rash enough to write books about them. If we examine the sections on *The Caretaker*, for instance, in the full-length studies of Pinter by Ronald Hayman and Simon Trussler, we find one writing that *The Caretaker* has been overrated as much as *The Birthday Party* has been underrated', while the other more than once refers to it as a 'great' play[6]; yet Trussler and Hayman join forces in condemning *The Homecoming*, a play for which Martin Esslin and others make high claims indeed.

Is Harold Pinter like the politician who can fool some of the people all of the time and all of the people some of the time, or are there deeper reasons for these differences of opinion? Is he simply a minor dramatist whose style and mannerisms are not to everybody's taste, or is it true, as Martin Esslin, Walter Kerr and a host of others affirm, that Pinter has succeeded in extending the frontiers of drama in a fundamental way?

It seems to me that the last of these views is the correct one, although it must be expressed with some reservations. It is certainly true that Pinter's plays call for a new critical approach, and (which is far more important) for a different kind of response on the part of audiences, but he sometimes does this by subtraction as much as by addition. If we have been brought up on the belief that we must understand a character's motives and background to get the maximum dramatic impact from any scene in which he appears, we have to perform a mental adjustment when Pinter's characters appear before us without this vital information. But Pinter's achievement here is rather to teach us to do without elements of the dramatic experience we had previously considered essential than to contribute anything positive. Furthermore, it is worth stressing that to say that a dramatist calls for a reappraisal of one's critical approaches is not the same thing as saying that his work is wholly without blemish. Unfortunately, many works of art which embody radical aesthetic principles are not particularly good as works of art, and there are undoubtedly moments in Pinter's drama where he falls back on old, familiar techniques in a manner that must disappoint all but his most uncritical admirers.

Having made these cautious disclaimers, let me go on to say that there are few occupations more fascinating than tracing the development of Pinter's work. There is a great temptation to use the plays as an excuse for excursions into anthropology or psychoanalysis, and readers may come to feel that I have not altogether avoided this temptation myself. Pinter undoubtedly plays his cards much closer to his subconscious than most dramatists, with the result that it is often difficult to explain, at any rational level, why his drama affects us so deeply. Nevertheless, I think it is possible, even if only obliquely at times, to give some account of what he is about as an artist, and why he deserves our close attention.

It is useful as a starting point to bear in mind one of Martin Esslin's observations:

> Pinter's first ambition was to write poetry; basically he has remained a lyric poet whose plays are structures of images of the world, very clear and precise and accurate images, which however, and that is the point, never aspire to be arguments, explanations, or even coherent stories[7].

Pinter is one of those artists who becomes fascinated by a single theme or image and explores it time after time, from one angle after another, in a succession of works. This is something we are familiar with in poetry or the visual arts, but it is less usual in the drama, which we normally look upon as a public rather than a personal medium. Nevertheless, it is one key to Pinter's cabinet of secrets. In approaching an author through a study of his recurrent imagery, one runs the risk of distorting his work by emphasizing minor features taken out of context, and by ignoring major features altogether. Omissions there certainly are in the following pages (I am conscious, for instance, of having neglected *The Dwarfs* and *Silence*, both important plays), but Pinter's repeated use of images is so central to his development that in this case the approach can, I think, be justified.

No-one would think it particularly odd if a painter produced a series of studies of a man reading a newspaper or magazine; but it may come as a mild surprise to discover that, among other things, this is what Pinter does in a sequence of plays from *The Room* to *The Homecoming*. In the opening scene of his first play, Rose fusses chattily around the room where Bert sits at the table, 'a magazine propped in front of him' (the photograph on the front cover of the printed edition shows him immersed in a comic strip version of *The Last of the Mohicans*). Clustered around this primary, visual image are most of the themes of the play—the warmth and comfort of the room contrasted with the inhospitable bleakness of the world outside the house, and the even more sinister menace of the basement downstairs; the indefinable relationship between Bert and Rose in which, as we shall find recurrently, a sexual or family bond is expressed obliquely in terms of food. Here is an extract from Rose's opening speech:

> But I think someone else has gone in now. I wouldn't like to live in that basement. Did you ever see the walls? They were running. This is all right for me. Go on, Bert. Have a bit more bread.
> [*She goes to the table and cuts a slice of bread.*]
> I'll have some cocoa on when you come back.
> [*She goes to the window and settles the curtain.*]
> No, this room's all right for me. I mean, you know where you are. When it's cold, for instance.
> [*She goes to the table.*]
> What about the rasher? Was it all right? It was a good one, I know, but not as good as the last lot I got in. It's the weather.   (p. 8)

Bert's failure to respond to Rose's conversational gambits is as significant as any spoken intervention: the magazine is principally a dramatic device to emphasize the barrier of silence between the two. We shall return to many of the themes mentioned by Rose; first let us trace the 'newspaper theme' in Pinter's subsequent work.

The Dumb Waiter opens with two men alone in a basement. As the action develops, it becomes apparent that they are hired killers in the employ of some nebulous agency, and the play ends with the discovery that this time Gus, the junior partner in the team, is himself the chosen victim. Ben and Gus are ambiguous figures: they carry guns and have power of life and death over their victims; and yet they are servants of an organization they cannot understand and cannot control. In the opening scene, Ben's marginal superiority over Gus is expressed visually by the fact that he is in possession of the newspaper:

> BEN *is lying on a bed, left, reading a paper.* GUS *is sitting on a bed, right, tying his shoelaces, with difficulty. Both are dressed in shirts, trousers and braces.*
> *Silence.*
> GUS *ties his laces, rises, yawns and begins to walk slowly to the door, left. He stops, looks down, and shakes his foot.*
> BEN *lowers his paper and watches him.* GUS *kneels and unties his shoelace and slowly takes off the shoe. He looks inside it and brings out a flattened matchbox. He shakes it and examines it. Their eyes meet.* BEN *rattles his paper and reads.* (p. 35)

The silent action continues: Gus discovers a 'flattened cigarette packet' in his other shoe, and we hear him having trouble with the plumbing of an off-stage lavatory. But eventually the dialogue begins, with Ben reading out a news item from his paper:

> BEN: What about this? Listen to this!
> [*He refers to the paper.*]
> A man of eighty-seven wanted to cross the road. But there was a lot of traffic, see? He couldn't see how he was going to squeeze through. So he crawled under a lorry.
> GUS: He what?
> BEN: He crawled under a lorry. A stationary lorry.
> GUS: No?
> BEN: The lorry started and ran over him. (p. 36)

A little later, Ben picks upon another arbitrary act of violence related in the newspaper: 'A child of eight killed a cat!' The events on-stage, and those read from the newspaper, seem chosen at random, in fact they are building up the dramatic background against which are set the pair's inability to control events and their confused attitude towards violence.

At the end of the play, Ben returns to the newspaper: with his extraordinary ability for building a theatrical climax out of the simplest elements, Pinter makes the empty shell of their earlier exchange reverberate with vague, indeterminate terror:

> BEN: Kaw!
> [*He picks up the paper and looks at it.*]
> Listen to this!
> [*Pause*]
> What about that, eh?
> [*Pause*]

Kaw!

[*Pause*]

Have you ever heard such a thing?

GUS: [*dully*]: Go on!   (p. 69)

It does not require much critical acumen to see that the newspaper theme is handled with greater dramatic subtlety than in *The Room*; it is not abandoned after the opening scene, and the material which is read out adds to the flavour of irrational violence which permeates the play.

The Birthday Party opens with a food-serving scene reminiscent of *The Room*, as Meg fusses around her husband:

MEG: I've got your cornflakes ready. [*She disappears and re-appears.*]

Here's your cornflakes. [*He rises and takes the plate from her, sits at the table, props up the paper and begins to eat. MEG enters by the kitchen door.*] Are they nice?

PETEY: Very nice.

MEG: I thought they'd be nice. [*She sits at the table.*] You got your paper?

PETEY: Yes.   (p. 9)

Petey talks where Bert was silent, and this gives Pinter scope for some characteristic dialogue:

MEG: What are you reading?

PETEY: Someone's just had a baby.

MEG: Oh, they haven't! Who?

PETEY: Some girl.

MEG: Who, Petey, who?

PETEY: I don't think you'd know her.

MEG: What's her name?

PETEY: Lady Mary Splatt.   (p. 11)

In this sequence, too, Pinter's comic inventiveness is firmly controlled by a deeper thematic unity. Meg is disturbed to learn that Lady Mary Splatt's child is a girl: 'I'd much rather have a little boy.' An attentive audience is prepared for the emergence, later in the scene, of Meg's mixture of maternal and sexual interest in Stanley, her unprepossessing boarder.

Act III, like Act I, is introduced by a conversation over the breakfast table between Meg and Petey; after the sinister events of the previous night, the repetition of the previous morning's routine is full of irony. Now, significantly, there is no food ('The two gentlemen had the last of the fry this morning'), and Petey's concentration on his newspaper marks his evasive attitude to Meg's conversation about Stanley.

It is significant, I think, that a piece of apparently deliberate mystification on Pinter's part which opens the intervening act has a visual link with the recurrent image of the newspaper reader: '*MCCANN is sitting at the table tearing a sheet of newspaper into five equal strips.*' McCann's action in tearing newspapers is never explained and remains wholly mysterious; but it is a disturbing reversal of the familiar Pinter opening, invested with private meaning and indicative of the destructive menace of the intruder upon the home. And in the final scene of the play when Petey, having witnessed Stanley's removal by Goldberg and McCann, returns to his breakfast table, the strips of torn paper fall from the newspaper he picks up to read, as a reminder of events he would rather forget.

The early Pinter, of course, is quite capable of opening a play without recourse to this image, and does so in *The Caretaker*; but it is back again, slightly subdued, in *A Slight Ache*, and seems to reach its culminating point in the opening of *The Homecoming*. It is a scene of beautiful economy, justifying quotation at length:

> *Evening.*
> LENNY *is sitting on the sofa with a newspaper, a pencil in his hand. He wears a dark suit. He makes occasional marks on the back page.*
> MAX *comes in, from the direction of the kitchen. He goes to sideboard, opens top drawer, rummages in it, closes it. He wears an old cardigan and a cap, and carries a stick. He walks downstage, stands, looks about the room.*
>
> MAX: What have you done with the scissors?
> [*Pause*]
> I said I'm looking for the scissors. What have you done with them?
> [*Pause*]
> Did you hear me? I want to cut something out of the paper.
> LENNY: I'm reading the paper.
> MAX: Not that paper. I haven't even read that paper. I'm talking about last Sunday's paper. I was just having a look at it in the kitchen.
> [*Pause*]
> Do you hear what I'm saying? I'm talking to you! Where's the scissors?
> LENNY: [*Looking up, quietly*]: Why don't you shut up, you daft prat? (p. 7)

By analysing the differences between this scene and the opening of *The Room* or *The Birthday Party* we can take a measure of Pinter's developing powers. At a superficial level the later scene is more 'realistic'; the reiterated mention of 'cornflakes' or 'rashers' would be out of place here. But beneath the surface the old preoccupation with personal images is as powerful as ever. Instead of the maternal figure of the earlier works, feeding and cosseting the male, we are now presented with a father-son relationship. Their rivalry is expressed by the cool self-possession of Lenny, 'reading the paper', in the face of Max's search for the scissors; but this is only one aspect of the scene. For Max comes in 'from the direction of the kitchen', and for all his masculine bluster he is the cook of the household. The reversal of normal roles hinted at by the involvement of a male in the domestic processes of the kitchen is closely linked to Max's ambiguous attitude towards his dead wife, who is mentioned fairly early in the proceedings:

> MAX: Mind you, she wasn't such a bad woman. Even though it made me sick just to look at her rotten stinking face, she wasn't such a bad bitch. I gave her the best bleeding years of my life, anyway.
> LENNY: Plug it, will you, you stupid sod, I'm trying to read the paper. (p. 9)

The structure of this opening scene is far more complex than anything we have examined hitherto, for the themes of the play are themselves more complex than anything Pinter had tackled satisfactorily in his earlier work. The exchange between Max and Lenny, set around the newspaper, the scissors and the recently finished meal, sets the tone for the unpredictable, and yet ultimately consistent, patterns of Max's reactions to the arrival of his son Ted on a fleeting visit from America with his wife Ruth. When Max first spots the couple the following morning he greets them with astonishing verbal violence:

> I've never had a whore under this roof before. Ever since your mother died. My word of honour.[*To* JOEY] Have you ever had a whore here? Has Lenny ever had a whore here? They come back from America, they bring the slopbucket with them. (p. 42)

A moment later, after a physical attack on his son Joey ('You're an old man', Joey had told his father), he reverts to what seems a feminine role:

> Teddy, why don't we have a nice cuddle and kiss, eh? Like the old days? What about a nice cuddle and kiss, eh? (p. 43)

The opening of the next act, unlike its predecessor, begins with an exchange of compliments about the quality of Max's cooking. But Max's innocent-sounding praise of Ruth, 'I've got the feeling you're a first-rate cook', soon leads to overt sexual territory; by the end of the act it has been agreed that Teddy is to return to America alone, while Ruth remains in the house, acting as a shared sexual partner and earning a living as a prostitute. In the figure of Ruth, half surrogate mother, half whore, there is plenty of material for Freudian analysis, but in terms of the play's dramatic structure, her instalment completes the ultimate defeat of Max, the male cook of the opening scene. Although he welcomed the proposal for Ruth's future, he is the first to suspect that the arrangement is not going to work. The play ends with a grotesque display of Max's humiliation:

> She won't . . . be adaptable!
> [*He begins to groan, clutches his stick, falls on to his knees by the side of her chair. His body sags. The groaning stops. His body straightens. He looks at her, still kneeling.*]
> I'm not an old man.
> [*Pause*]
> Do you hear me?
> [*He raises his face to her.*]
> Kiss me.
> [*She continues to touch* JOEY's *head, lightly.*]
> [LENNY *stands, watching.*] (pp. 81–82)

We have moved beyond our initial study of Pinter's use of the newspaper image; and indeed in *The Homecoming* Pinter seems to have carried it to the point of total integration with the structure of the play; from now on the various subsidiary images with which we have seen it linked exist in their own right and independently. The barrier between one character and another suggested in the earlier play by the interposed newspaper or magazine gives way to the infinitely more subtle studies of two characters separated from one another by memory; the preparation and delivery of food, as an image for sexual relationship, moves to the foreground and casts off its earlier associations with the fussing woman and the newspaper reader.

I have begun with a study of this apparently trivial aspect of Pinter's work not simply because it shows so clearly how the dramatist returns to the same image like a prospector to his mine, tunnelling beneath the surface until the whole seam is exhausted, but because in this case the image is obviously a private one, not susceptible to interpretation at any archetypal level. This is surely a hint to the over-enthusiastic symbol-hunter that even when Pinter's images do seem to touch on more universal themes familiar in mythology or psychoanalysis, we should do well not to dwell on this aspect of their nature at the expense of missing their connection to the rest of Pinter's artistry.

For instance, the theme of blindness or afflicted vision is an important one in Pinter's early work, but it would probably be unwise to identify it too closely with the traditional use of blindness as a poetic image, laden with overtones at times of supernatural wisdom, at times of symbolic castration, which stretches back to Sophocles' *Oedipus* and beyond. In Pinter's plays it is much more personal and inexplicable, and like the opening gambit we have already studied, it gives way in time to a new image.

At the end of *The Room* it is used somewhat crudely and melodramatically. We have seen how Ruth treats the room of the title as a haven of security shielding her from the outside world; during Bert's absence she is subjected to a series of attacks upon this security. First there is a visit from some prospective tenants who, alarmingly, have been told her room is available, then Mr Kidd (whether or not he is actually the landlord is a debated point that has kept Pinter critics awake at nights) returns with the news that a man in the basement insists on seeing her when Mr Hudd is away. The play builds up to a climax with the arrival of this figure: '*enter a blind Negro.*' This moment is certainly effective theatrically, and the enigmatic bond of knowledge between him and Ruth marks the first appearance of Pinter's fascination with the secret world of the remembered past:

RILEY: Your father wants you to come home.
        [*Pause*]
ROSE: Home?
RILEY: Yes.
ROSE: Home? Go now. Come on. It's late. It's late.
RILEY: To come home.
ROSE: Stop it. I can't take it. What do you want? What do you want?
RILEY: Come home, Sal.
        [*Pause*]
ROSE: What did you call me?   (p. 30)

Rose seems on the verge of capitulation when Bert returns from his expedition in the van. At last he breaks his silence: 'I got back all right.' There is a strong vein of sexuality in the description of his journey: 'I caned her along. She was good', he remarks . . . 'She went with me.' Only then does he see the negro, and exclaiming 'Lice!' he strikes him brutally, and perhaps kills him. At this point, the play ends with a second blinding:

Rose stands clutching her eyes.
ROSE: Can't see. I can't see. I can't see. (p. 32)

It is a disturbing enough conclusion, with a succession of violent, sharply visualized actions culminating in a stark moment of physical anguish. I find it less than wholly satisfying, however, because blindness is a theme introduced only in the final scene of the play. Compare it with the way in which the final close-up shot of Disson's staring, unresponsive eyes in *Tea Party* (examined in Chapter II) is foreshadowed by the recurrent binding of his eyes with a chiffon scarf, and the manner in which that, in its turn, is linked to the disintegration of his sense of sexual adequacy. In *A Slight Ache*, too, Edward's eventual humiliation is hinted at earlier by that 'slight ache' in his eyes[8].

It is in *The Birthday Party* that Pinter's most satisfying treatment of the theme of eyes devoid of sight emerges. When Stanley first appears, unshaven and scruffy, for his boarding-house breakfast, he is wearing his glasses, and for all his unwholesome appearance he is cocky and full of self-assurance. Throughout the play his moments of vulnerability are indicated, with great precision, by the removal of his glasses. In the following passage, Stanley is talking of his short-lived career (it may be, imagined career) as a concert pianist. It began well ('I had a unique touch') with his first concert at Lower Edmonton. But he has bitter memories of the sequel. 'They carved me up', he says:

> It was all arranged, it was all worked out. My next concert. Somewhere else it was. In winter. I went down there to play. Then, when I got there, the hall was closed, the place was shuttered up, not even a caretaker. They'd locked it up.
> [*Takes off his glasses and wipes them on his pyjama jacket.*]
> A fast one. They pulled a fast one. I'd like to know who was responsible for that. [*Bitterly*] All right, Jack, I can take a tip. They want me to crawl down on my bended knees. Well I can take a tip . . . any day of the week. [*He replaces his glasses, then looks at MEG.*] Look at her. You're just an old piece of rock cake, aren't you? (p. 23)

When the mysterious intruders Goldberg and McCann first arrive, it is significant that Stanley is momentarily without his spectacles as he washes his face at the kitchen sink[9]. Inevitably, the interrogation which the intruders mount against Stanley involves the forcible removal of his glasses[10]. And Act II moves towards its climax when, in the eerie birthday party which gives the play its title, Stanley is persuaded to surrender his glasses in a game of blind man's buff; while his eyes are bound with a scarf (an image that recurs in *Tea Party*), McCann deliberately breaks Stanley's glasses, 'snapping the frames'[11]. From that moment he is conquered; in his chilling final appearance, neatly dressed and apparently in a catatonic state of speechlessness, he clutches the broken glasses in his hand, and Petey's suggestion that the frames can be mended with Sellotape[12] is a pathetically inadequate response to the disaster that has overtaken his friend.

In Pinter's developing exploration of this theme the loss of sight increasingly represents a mental rather than a physical state; after *Tea Party* he dispenses with this external manifestation of breakdown altogether, and without reducing the strong visual content of his closing scenes, he is able to reveal the essence of human desolation without recourse to this symbol of physical distress. Max kneeling before Ruth in the presence of his two sons, raising his face to her and appealing 'Kiss me', or Deeley sobbing 'very quietly' after his wife's final speech in *Old Times*, are compact images so wholly related to what has gone before that they cannot, like the image of blindness, be pursued from one play to another.

In the case of the newspaper theme the progress was mainly technical, as the theme became steadily more involved with the play as a whole; in the case of the movement from the early use of blindness as a final image towards the powerful closing scenes of the later plays we encounter another aspect of Pinter's development which can be seen in one feature after another of his work. It might be described as Pinter's journey to the interior. It is not so much that he abandons the mystifying blows of fate in the earlier plays as that the mystery steadily moves within. Instead of being an unexplained part of the world outside his characters, the destructive forces have become an aspect, equally inexplicable in the long run, of their own psychology. This 'interiorization' of themes will be explored in more detail later; but it is something that can hardly be neglected whatever aspect of Pinter's work one happens to be studying.

There are numerous themes, large and small, that could be traced from Pinter's earliest plays and throughout his subsequent work. There is, for instance, the obsession with parental and brother–sister, brother–brother relationships. In *The Room* we find Mr Kidd extraordinarily vague about his background:

> I think my mother was a Jewess. Yes, I wouldn't be surprised to learn she was a Jewess. She didn't have many babies. (p. 15)

And there is the curious message delivered to Rose by the negro: 'Your father wants you to come home'; we shall return to it shortly. Martin Esslin has spelt out in great detail, sometimes more fascinating than convincing, the significance of the relationship between the two brothers and the old tramp in terms of family relationships in *The Caretaker*[13]. This particular strand in Pinter's imaginative development seems to reach its flowering in the rich and subtle network of sibling, parent–child and male–female relationships in *The Homecoming*, where the confusing patterns of alternative acceptance and rejection are as complex as any R D Laing case-history.

There is, too, Pinter's treatment of female sexuality, which develops through the plays almost in the manner ascribed by psychologists to the development of the male attitude to the female sex. First come the cosy, possessive mother-figures, purveying food, comfort and security, and yet doomed to rejection, in *The Room* and *The Birthday Party*. Then we find the adolescent fantasy-image of the whore, shameless, inventive, and readily available, while remaining, like all fantasies, ultimately elusive. She is a figure foreshadowed in *A Slight Ache* and studied with increasing subtlety in *A Night Out*, *Night School*, *The Lover*, and *Tea Party*, to achieve her apotheosis in *The Homecoming* where Ruth, as if to emphasize the point, replaces the mother in the male household[14]. Finally, in his most recent and mature work, Pinter presents us with women who have rejected the role of simple sex-object for their male partner and become independent individuals with their own scheme of memories and their own intense inner experience.

Another theme which has drawn much attention to itself is the question of verification, or the relationship between one or more person's account of an event and the actual event itself (insofar as that can be determined). It will not be traced in detail here; like most of the themes under review it changes its nature as Pinter's dramaturgy marches towards the interior; in the later plays the alternative versions of events offered by the characters have become one aspect of memory. The past, true or false, real or imagined, comes to have less importance for its own sake and becomes instead the vital material of a character's present existence.

One recurrent theme which I do wish to discuss in some detail is Pinter's fascination with the naming process; this will lead us into other areas which I believe to lie at the heart of Pinter's distinctive quality as a dramatist. And it will touch upon another important topic, his use of language.

Nomen omen, the Romans used to say, to indicate that what a person or thing is called is mystically linked to its inner being and destiny; and we recall the old tale of one Rumpelstiltskin, whose evil power was destroyed as soon as his name was known. Pinter's characters seem to react to the use of their names with something of the same ancient superstition. As so often, *The Room* contains the first sketch for a theme which recurs, with increasing assurance, throughout his later work. When Mr and Mrs Sands call on Rose in search of the landlord, there is confusion over the name of the man they are seeking; Rose's assurance that the landlord's name is Mr Kidd leaves Mr Sands unsatisfied. This confusion is elaborated a few moments later when Rose formally introduces herself as 'Mrs Hudd':

MR SANDS: . . . You're the wife of the bloke you mentioned then?
MRS SANDS: No, she isn't. That was Mr Kidd.
MR SANDS: Was it? I thought it was Hudd.
MRS SANDS: No, it was Kidd. Wasn't it, Mrs Hudd?
ROSE: That's right. The landlord.
MRS SANDS: No, not the landlord. The other man.
ROSE: Well, that's his name. He's the landlord.
MR SANDS: Who?
ROSE: Mr Kidd.
                 [*Pause*]
MR SANDS: Is he?
MRS SANDS: Maybe there are two landlords.
                 [*Pause*]
MR SANDS: That'll be the day.   (pp. 18–19)

This passage is a good example of Pinter's early style. Apparently almost wholly devoid of meaningful content, it achieves a fine comic effect through carefully orchestrated repetition, as the initial misunderstanding gradually reduces language to the point of total absurdity with each character grimly hanging on to his own viewpoint until the apparent deadlock is broken by a skilfully timed but inappropriate *cliché*: 'That'll be the day'. But behind the confusion over names there lurks a deeper confusion of identities: the question of whether or not Mr Kidd is the landlord (or, if you like, whether the real name of the landlord is Mr

Kidd) seems linked with this shadowy character's own inability to define himself ('I think my mum was a Jewess').

The monosyllabic surnames are bandied about, telling us nothing about their owners. But first names are something else. They are personal, not collective, and only privileged persons are entitled to use them. Mrs Sands seems to dominate her husband by the way she wields his ugly nickname. Toddy. His naming of her is a conscious act of rebellion in the course of an argument over whether or not he should sit down:

MRS SANDS: You don't look one thing or another standing up.
MR SANDS: I'm quite all right, Clarissa.
ROSE: Clarissa? What a pretty name.
MRS SANDS: Yes, it is nice, isn't it? My father and mother gave it to me. (p. 18)

Nothing could be more absurd than Mrs Sands' reply to Rose's compliment; but paradoxically, it is only absurd because of its truth. First names are intimate things, part of the parental endowment; that is why we are cautious about their use.

With these earlier scenes in mind, it is interesting to turn to the final scene of *The Room*. When the blind negro first enters, hostilities commence with Rose's refusal to acknowledge her name:

RILEY: Mrs Hudd?
ROSE: You just touched a chair. Why don't you sit in it? (p. 28)

Rose's unfriendly reception continues as the negro takes a seat and 'looks about the room':

RILEY: My name is Riley.
ROSE: I don't care if it's—What? That's not your name. That's not your name. You've got a grown-up woman in this room, do you hear? (p. 28)

The negro reacts calmly to Rose's abuse, which reaches its climax when she accuses him of pestering the landlord:

We're settled down here, cosy, quiet, and our landlord thinks the world of us, we're his favourite tenants, and you come in and drive him up the wall, and drag my name into it! What did you mean by dragging my name into it, and my husband's name? How did you know what our name was? (p. 29)

But he delivers his message, in the passage already quoted: 'Your father wants you to come home'. And this is the moment when the negro delivers the blow that all but defeats Rose. He calls her by her first name:

RILEY: Come home, Sal.
ROSE: Don't call me that.
RILEY: Come, now.
ROSE: Don't call me that.
RILEY: So now you're here.
ROSE: Not Sal. (p. 30)

Unlike Clarissa Sands, the epitome of ordinary womanhood, acknowledging the pretty name her father and mother gave her, Rose has abandoned her parental endowment; her anxious fear of the world outside the room is intimately linked to the terror aroused in her when the negro enters with a 'message' from home. Even in this first play of Pinter's, the interaction of the past upon the present plays a vital part; the negro's use of the name 'Sal' touches a chord which echoes throughout Pinter's later work.

In *The Birthday Party* there are some unremarkable switches from first name to surname and back to accentuate the shifting moods as the two intruders set to work on their intimidation of Stanley, and at one part he is accused of using a false name; Goldberg himself turns out to have no less than three first names[15].

In *The Caretaker* the tramp claims that the name on his Insurance Card, Bernard Jenkins, is only his 'assumed' name. His real name is 'Davies—Mac Davies'[16], an evasion which links him with Rose and Stanley in the earlier plays, both of whom appear to have abandoned their names in an attempt to escape from their past. In *A Slight Ache* the turning-point of the play is marked, in a memorable Pinterism, by Flora's adoption of the silent match-seller: 'I'm going to keep you, you dreadful chap, and call you Barnabas.'[17]

A high point of Pinter's exploration of the nomenclature theme can be found, I think, in *The Homecoming*. We have already received a strong hint that we are on familiar territory in Lenny's encounter with Ruth in Act I. An argument arises over whether Ruth should surrender a glass of water to Lenny. She has consumed 'quite sufficient, in my own opinion', Lenny tells her:

RUTH: Not in mine, Leonard.
     [Pause]
LENNY: Don't call me that, please.
RUTH: Why not?
LENNY: That's the name my mother gave me.   (p. 33)

This reminds us, of course, of the scene in *The Room* where Clarissa Sands is complimented on the name 'her father and mother gave her'; but the same idea is used here with much greater subtlety, for the parallel between Ruth and the mother is stressed continually throughout the play and eventually, in her new role as a woman shared by the members of the household, she is to replace the mother. And almost at the end of the play, Teddy is on the verge of departure when his wife calls out to him:

Eddie.
[TEDDY turns. Pause.]
Don't become a stranger.   (p. 80)

This hitherto unspoken private name, differing only slightly from his normal one (he has been called Teddy, and occasionally Ted, by his family) suddenly opens up a world of unsuspected intimacy between husband and wife. As so often in Pinter's work, examination of a single scene could occupy a whole chapter, and the questions raised by these five words of Ruth seem to me immense.

Martin Esslin takes the view that Ruth and Teddy's marriage has failed (he is, after all, an academic), and that is why she acquiesces in the barely concealed obscenity of the family's proposals for her future. But Teddy and Ruth have 'overslept' when they appear at the head of the stairs after their first night in the family household; Joey failed to 'go the whole hog' after two hours in the bedroom with Ruth[18]; and Max, as we have seen, quickly reaches the desperate conclusion that 'she won't . . . be adaptable'. Just as significantly, in Pinter's private imagery, Teddy has calmly and deliberately eaten a cheese roll which Lenny had prepared with loving care for himself. For all the extraordinary events of the play the reserved and aloof Teddy, in the persona of Eddie, seems to maintain a sexual bond with Ruth to which the others never attain and never will. In an eerie sort of way his departure without his wife represents a sort of triumph for him. Eddie, we feel, is intact; and Teddy, the son and brother, has used his 'homecoming' to liberate himself from his indefinable burden of the past.

Pinter has often been praised for his 'ear' for realistic dialogue. But he goes far beyond incorporating the sort of off-beat phrases we are continually hearing in pubs and buses into his plays for simple comic effect. Each of his characters uses a vocabulary and sentence structure so full of idiosyncracies that it amounts to a private system of language, revealing inner obsessions rather than in the way that a speaker struggling with a foreign language gives us some idea of his own tongue by way of his peculiar variations in grammatical usage and vocabulary. It is true of course that the idea of a 'subtext' lurking behind the spoken words and revealing the characters' inner feelings has been with us at least since the time of Chekhov[19]; but Pinter carries the process one stage further. The unconscious workings of the mind revealed (if that is the right word) in Pinter's 'subtext' clarify nothing for his audiences. Their language systems hint at mysteries which even the author does not claim to be able to unravel. To pursue our earlier analogy, it is as if they are foreigners whose peculiar speech points back to a language of which we are completely ignorant.

It is against this context of Pinter's use of language in general, I think, that his fascination with the naming process is so important. A name is something shared; it exists *outside* a language-system and cannot be wholly subordinated to the obsessions of one person. When a Pinter character calls another character by his or her name, there is a sudden moment of human contact. This is why the climax of so many of his plays is reached with the utterance of a first name held back until that moment.

Food, as we have seen, plays an important role in Pinter's drama, and it is interesting that whenever the subject comes up the food is *named* with great particularity and emphasis. There are Meg's cornflakes and Goldberg's gefilte fish in *The Birthday Party*; there is Lenny's cheese roll in *The Homecoming*. In *The Dumb Waiter* destiny itself appears in the form of orders for ever more exotically named meals reaching Ben and Gus from the outer world. In a famous sequence the two, confronted with an order for 'Macaroni Pastitsio' and 'Ormitha Macarounada' do their best with inadequate resources:

> GUS: [*calling up the hatch*] Three McVitie and Price! One Lyons Red Label! One Smith's Crisps! One Eccles cake! One Fruit and Nut!
> BEN: Cadbury's.
> GUS: [*up the hatch*]Cadbury's.

101

BEN: [*handing the milk*] One bottle of milk.
GUS: [*up the hatch*] One bottle of milk! Half a pint! [*He looks at the label*] Express Dairy!
[*He puts the bottle in the box*] (p. 58)

One is tempted to recall that a traditional scene in ancient Greek comedy depicted the arrival of a cook reciting a lengthy list of the delicacies he was preparing for a banquet. The gap between the essential nature of food, the primal source of life and energy, and the ludicrous brand-names assigned to it in sophisticated society, is a fundamental source of comedy; but food is important also because, as something handled and prepared by one person and passed on to another for consumption, it involves human beings in an intimate relationship. Food, like a name, is shared; it is something else which exists outside language.

From the insufficiency of Ben and Gus, brilliantly effective on a comic level, we pass to a scene in *Landscape* where Pinter uses the same image with vivid intensity at the climax of Duff's sequence of memories. He recalls Beth standing in the hall of the empty house, banging the gong as if for a meal:

It's bullshit. Standing in an empty hall banging a bloody gong. There's no one to listen. No one'll hear. There's not a soul in the house. Except me. There's nothing for lunch. There's nothing cooked. No stew. No pie. No greens. No joint. Fuck all. (p. 28)

Instead of the packaged and processed foodstuffs mustered by Ben and Gus, Duff invokes the food prepared at home in the kitchen, the meat and vegetables with which the woman, as cook, fulfils a role as elemental as her sexual partnership with the male. Out of a succession of negatives, followed by the sharp explosion of a sexual oath, Pinter has fashioned an extraordinary cry of despair, unique and terrible.

A study of recurrent themes and images can carry us a certain way towards an appreciation of Pinter's distinctive qualities. But it is equally necessary to look at a play in its entirety, to see how these images are handled in terms of overall dramatic structure. For if there is one feature of his work that Pinter himself has stressed time after time, it is that the dramatist is the person who puts it all together:

... as far as I'm concerned, my characters and I inhabit the same world. The only difference between them and me is that they don't arrange and select. I do the donkey work[20].

The early plays have been studied so exhaustively by other critics that it may be more rewarding in the case of Pinter to restrict our detailed analysis to two of the later plays, *Landscape* and *Old Times*; in the study of both plays we shall refer back to the earlier work, and in particular some important features in *A Slight Ache* will be mentioned.

Landscape, which appeared with its companion *Silence* at the Aldwych Theatre in 1969, is a play which seems on first examination to offer little or no dramatic development in the conventional sense of the words. A man and a woman are seated in the kitchen of a country house, talking spasmodically. Not only do they never move; the opening stage direction emphasizes what is made abundantly clear in the dialogue that follows, namely that their alternating speeches are in no real sense a conversation:

> DUFF *refers normally to* BETH, *but does not appear to hear her voice.*
> BETH *never looks at* DUFF, *and does not appear to hear his voice.*
>
> (p. 8)

Coming from the author of plays bursting with effective *coups de théâtre*, this seemed to some critics to be an indication of diminishing dramatic powers and the obvious influence, the later plays of Samuel Beckett, was frequently mentioned to account for this change of direction. Such works as Beckett's *Play* doubtless have their connection with the genesis of *Landscape*; nevertheless, it is quintessentially a Pinter play, developing, compressing and intensifying themes that appeared in his earlier work and containing them inside a structure that is beautifully controlled and anything but static.

The two characters are in early middle age; from Duff it becomes evident that the couple were formerly servants to one Mr Sykes ('a gloomy bugger', as he remarks); now they have apparently inherited his house, where they live alone. But their present situation is far less important than the memory-patterns inside which they live and to which their speech constantly refers. Hence the immobility of the play, in visual terms, is dramatically appropriate, indicating a kind of paralysis in their relationship. Duff (as the stage direction quoted above suggests) is concerned for Beth; when he talks about recent events, he is seeking to share his experience with her:

> The dog's gone. I didn't tell you.
> [*Pause*]
> I had to shelter under a tree for twenty minutes yesterday. Because of the rain. I meant to tell you. With some youngsters. I didn't know them.
> [*Pause*]
> Then it eased. A downfall. I walked up as far as the pond. Then I felt a couple of big drops. Luckily I was only a few yards from the shelter. I sat down in there. I meant to tell you. (p. 10)

As Duff's memory moves from his recent doings (a conversation with a stranger in a pub is a highlight of his solitary existence) back into the past, Beth remains in his thoughts:

> You were a first-rate housekeeper when you were young. Weren't you? I was very proud. You never made a fuss, you never got into a state, you went about your work. He could rely on you. He did.
>
> (p. 18)

After he had returned from 'a trip to the north' with his employer, he 'had something to say' to his wife:

> I waited, I didn't say it then, but I'd made up my mind to say it, I'd decided I would say it, and I did say it, the next morning. Didn't I?
> [*Pause*]
> I told you that I'd let you down. I'd been unfaithful to you. (p. 19)

While Duff, in this way, constantly moulds his patterns of speech around Beth, she never so much as mentions him; all her speech (an 'internal monologue', as Martin Esslin appropriately describes it)[21] revolves around a brief affair, and in particular a lyrical moment of love-making on a beach.

The identity of the lover is a minor but almost wholly irrelevant mystery. It may have been Mr Sykes, thus giving point and dramatic irony to Duff's memory of the high regard in which he held Beth, and a sequence of references to a 'blue dress' which he gave her; it may have been a stranger, encountered while Duff and his employer were on their trip to the north (thus giving added significance to the recurrent mention of the home-baked bread which Beth had with her on Duff's return); or it may have been Duff himself, at a time long before his infidelity. The latter, we are told, is the one that Pinter himself inclined to after he had written the play[27].

Although there is no contact between the two at a conscious level, their dialogue is linked by a delicate counterpoint of contrasted images. Beth opens the play by talking of the sea, the beach and the dune where 'her man slept':

> I would like to stand by the sea. It is there.
> [*Pause*]
> I have. Many times. It's something I cared for. I've done it.
> [*Pause*]
> I'll stand on the beach. On the beach. Well . . . it was very fresh. But it was hot, in the dunes. But it was so fresh, on the shore. I loved it very much. (p. 9)

Duff brings the imagery down to earth by describing his walk 'as far as the pond'. Beth talks of her lover watching her watering and arranging some flowers[22]; a little later Duff is trying to persuade Beth to spend some time in the garden, 'You'd like that':

> I've put in some flowers. You'd find it pleasant. Looking at the flowers. You could cut a few if you liked. Bring them in. No-one would see you. There's no-one there. (p. 16)

While Duff relates his visit to the pub, Beth revives her memories of a 'hotel' where she went with her lover.

Like contrasting themes weaving their way in and out of a piece of music, the reminiscences of Beth and Duff merge and separate, linked by a continuous flow of recurrent detail—the beach, the pond, the dog, the tiny but all-important detail of the bag with its home-baked bread:

> BETH: He said he knew a very desolate beach, that no-one else in the world knew, and that's where we are going.
> DUFF: I was very gentle to you. I was kind to you, that day. I knew you'd had a shock, so I was gentle with you. I held your arm on the way back from the pond. You put your hands on my face and kissed me.
> BETH: All the food I had in my bag I had cooked myself, or prepared myself. I had baked the bread myself. (p. 22)

The order is not logical or narrative, but poetic, a glimpse of two separate consciousnesses through the window of language, balanced in an alternating structure of speech and silence. The climax, too, is not a climax of events reached in a temporal sequence, but an existential climax of contrasted experience. Duff's language becomes more and more violently masculine as the play progresses; before the final speech, full of overt sexual reference, he describes in vigorous detail the daily routine of a cellarman, a topic which developed during his conversation with the stranger in the pub. Beth's memories of the early-morning dew contrast with the picture of the cellarman going about his subterranean duties:

BETH: I opened the door and went out. There was no-one about. The sun was shining. Wet, I mean wetness, all over the ground.
DUFF: A cellarman is the man responsible. He's the earliest up in the morning. Give the draymen a hand with the barrels. Down the slide through the cellarflaps. Lower them by rope to the racks. Rock them on the belly, put a rim up them, use balance and leverage, hike them up onto the racks.
BETH: Still misty, but thinner, thinning.
DUFF: The bung is on the vertical, in the bunghole. Spile the bung. Hammer the spile through the centre of the bung. That lets the air through the bung, down the bunghole, lets the beer breathe.
BETH: Wetness all over the air. Trees like feathers. (p. 25)

It is a little reminiscent of Bert's account of his journey in *The Room* ('I caned her along'); but here the sexual analogies are subtler and set in a richer context. At one level of contrast, we are presented with Beth's dreamy abstractions; at another, with the intimation that all Duff's masculine bluster is an evasion, leading up to but also staving off the inevitable themes of his last two speeches. Soon the emptiness of his life will be revealed in the speech already quoted: 'There's nothing for lunch. There's nothing cooked. No stew. No pie. No greens. No joint. Fuck all.'

Duff's final speech erupts into coarse violence as he describes how he tore off Beth's chain with its thimbles and key, her insignia as housekeeper, and 'booted the gong down the hall'. The speech continues, with the banging of the gong, announcing that food is ready, merging with a furious sense of sexual desire and leading, after a silence, to Beth's final speech:

DUFF: . . . you'll plead with me like a woman, I'll bang the gong on the floor, if the sound is too flat, lacks resonance, I'll hang it back on its hook, bang you against it swinging, gonging, waking the place up, calling them all for dinner, lunch is up, bring out the bacon, bang your lovely head, mind the dog doesn't swallow the thimble, slam—
Silence
BETH: He lay above me and looked down at me. He supported my shoulder.
[*Pause*]
So tender his touch on my neck. So softly his kiss on my cheek.
[*Pause*]

My hand on his rib.

[*Pause*]

So sweetly the sand over me. Tiny the sand on my skin.

[*Pause*]

So silent the sky in my eyes. Gently the sound of the tide.

[*Pause*]

Oh my true love I said.   (p. 29–30)

If these final words are deeply moving, it is because everything in the play leads to this expression of the eternal gulf between the two characters. But is is hardly an exaggeration to say that almost every major feature of Pinter's work is compressed into this climactic sequence. To justify this latter remark, it is necessary to go back on our tracks.

Pinter's early plays abounded in unexplained, irrational acts of violence, treated in a manner that earned them the title 'comedies of menace'[23]. At first the playwright introduced an outside agent to produce this effect by breaking up the warmth and security established in a single room; such agents are the blind negro in *The Room*, the messages emerging from the lift-shaft and the speaking tube in *The Dumb Waiter*, Goldberg and McCann in *The Birthday Party*. In *The Caretaker* the meance is largely reversed, in that it is the intruder in the shape of Davies who suffers and is finally ejected from the home.

In *A Slight Ache*, with the benefit of hindsight, we can spot a subtle shift in the nature of the 'menace' to the stability and security of the main characters. This play, by no means a major one in the Pinter canon, is nevertheless important because in it the dramatist can be seen moving towards the themes of his mature work. A mysterious 'intruder' is still central to the plot: it is the silent matchseller standing at the bottom of the garden who so unnerves Edward. But fairly soon in the play, a significant change in the role of the intruder takes place, for the matchseller is *invited in* to the house by Edward, who sends his wife out to fetch him[24]. And when he arrives, the havoc that he causes results, not from anything he says, but from the fact that he says nothing at all. In the face of this relentless silence Edward talks and talks, reaching total incoherence and personal breakdown more or less simultaneously at the end. (The play was written for radio where, as Martin Esslin points out, the role of the matchseller, represented by pure silence, is much more effective than in the stage version.)[25] In short, Edward's breakdown can hardly be said to be engineered by an external force; it is something he brings, almost deliberately, upon himself.

The reaction of Edward's wife to the matchseller is no less interesting. She begins by protesting against Edward's agitation: 'he's a poor, harmless old man.' 'He's an old man. You won't ... be rough with him?'[26] But in her scene alone with him, the seemingly placid surface of her life is ruffled, and old memories stir:

Between ourselves, were you ever a poacher? I had an encounter with a poacher once. It was a ghastly rape, the brute.   (pp. 30–31)

The rape itself is described:

I went to him, he rose, I fell, my pony took off, down to the valley, I saw the sky through the trees, blue. Up to my ears in mud. It was a desperate battle.   (p. 31)

As is always the case when one of Pinter's characters travels into the past, there is no determining the truth of Flora's story; but of her sexual arousal there can be no doubt. We find the conjunction of sexual imagery with a vivid glimpse of natural scenery; not for the first time Pinter introduces a theme or technique in a comic context, to return to it later within a deeper scheme of values; we can compare the passage quoted with the use of natural scenery in *Landscape*, where images of sea and sand blend continually with Beth's memories of her love-making.

Soon Flora is making intimate enquiries of the matchseller ('Have you ever . . . stopped a woman?') and associating his filthy appearance with her memories or the poacher episode: 'You haven't been rolling in mud, have you?' She plans to clean him up:

> All you need is a bath. A lovely lathery bath. And a good scrub. A
> lovely lathery scrub.   (p. 32)

She dubs him with her private first name, Barnabas; and the play ends rather unsatisfactorily with her handing Edward the tray of matches as she leads 'Barnabas' into the garden.

Despite its amusing touches, it is hardly vintage Pinter; but it deserves attention because in it we find Pinter rehearsing themes which are to gather strength later. The matchseller, with his negative role as the projection of the fantasies of the other two characters, is unlike the mysterious intruders from an alien world in his earliest plays; later, the disruptive work is done either by figures like Teddy and Ruth in *The Homecoming*, characters on the same plane of existence as their fellows in the play, or else, as in *Landscape*, by images of memory acting without external stimulus. In *Old Times*, memory and intruders have reached such a level of identification that it becomes meaningless to ask whether Anna, Kate's old friend on a flying visit, 'exists' or is merely a figment of the memory-patterns that compose the play.

In either case, the characters are now attacked by something deep within themselves. Pinter gives us a series of blustering males, full of assertive self-confidence, who end in a state of numb despair. Edward in *A Slight Ache*, with his constant emphasis on physical prowess, is one such; there is Disson in *Tea Party*, Max in *The Homecoming*, Duff in *Landscape*, Deeley in *Old Times*. In each play they are balanced by a female figure whose role is far more passive and yet by the final scene has proved immensely powerful. It is as if Pinter continues to view all human action as arbitrary, irrational, and unpredictable, but now attributes a different kind of irrationality to male and female. Sudden eruptions of violence are characteristic of the man—Edward's savage onslaught upon the wasp in the early scenes of *A Slight Ache,* Max's physical and verbal outbursts, Duff's final speech in *Landscape*. Equally inexplicable in the female is the act of sexual surrender; Flora initiates Pinter's study of the 'whore' figure who encapsulates the mystery of woman's supreme act of submission when paradoxically, by giving herself completely, she asserts her superior power.

We can see that once the figure of the mysterious intruder is swept away, the dramatic structure allows the two sides of human irrationality, male and female, to interact. In *A Slight Ache* the final substitution of the matchseller for Edward in Flora's affections is less than wholly successful in theatrical terms because the crucial scenes which have preceded it present either the man or the woman alone with the matchseller. One can speculate, of course, about the failure of Edward and Flora's marital relationship, but Pinter does not give us much encouragement to do so.

One problem which inevitably confronts a writer concerned with the areas of experience which surface in Pinter's plays is that of containing arbitrary and irrational events within an ordered artistic structure. Each succeeding speech or action in a Pinter play is unpredictable, and yet goes towards completing the pattern of the whole[27]. In the earlier plays the sense of artistic unity was largely achieved by 'foreshadowing' the arrival of the intruder and thus making his inexplicable behaviour part of a larger whole. One could trace, for instance, the references to the mysterious occupant of the basement which builds up dramatic tension in *The Room*, or the intermittent references to the strangers looking for accommodation in Act I of *The Birthday Party*, balanced by Stanley's announcement to a frightened Meg that 'they're coming in a van' and 'looking for someone'[28]. In *The Homecoming*, the anticipation of the final scene hinges a shade less on the actual intruder (if that is the right description of Ruth), and rather more on the tortuous relationship between Max, with his blustering aggression and ambivalent memories of his late wife, and his three sons and their equally complex attitudes towards the female sex. The disturbance which Ruth's presence causes jolts this relationship and brings it to a point of crisis. The play's abruptly shocking conclusion is prepared and defined by the swift changes in direction which characterize the emotions and attitudes of Max and, to a lesser extent, the rest of his family.

In *Landscape* similarly the irrationality of human conduct which, as we have suggested, is separated into its male and female elements, is contained within an appropriate and satisfying artistic structure. It is a play of experience and not of events, in which memory performs a role comparable to that of the physical intruder in the earlier plays. The contrapuntal patterns of imagery serve the same function as the foreshadowing of events in the earlier plays.

In *Landscape*, then, the development of a relationship is carried forward by language, and it comes as no surprise to discover Pinter in the final speeches of the play refashioning themes which have long preoccupied him in his study of the two worlds inside and outside language. Duff's frantic cry of 'lunch is up, bring out the bacon' makes the analogy between food and sexuality more distinct than ever before, while the last words of the play recall the most profound of all naming ceremonies, the definitive moment of freedom from the name one's father and mother gave one: 'Oh my true love I said.'

Pinter is a Janus-headed dramatist, looking forward and back simultaneously, and of no play is this more true than his recent full-length work *Old Times*. When *Landscape* first appeared, it seemed to me that by converting the overt violence of the earliest plays into opposing aspects of male and female psychology, and by cutting down physical action on the stage to vanishing point, Pinter had reached a stage of development beyond which he could hardly pass. I was wrong. *Old Times* leads into new territory at the same time as it looks back, refining and commenting upon themes that have gone before.

Some less gentle readers may already have become impatient with my definition of *Landscape* as an expression of the male and female character. Was any love affair ever so lyrically unclouded as the one remembered by Beth? Those simple images of sea and sand, of sun and sky, are occasionally only a hairsbreadth away from novelettish sentimentality. They deny as much as they affirm of the true nature of sexual experience, and although it is clear she is idealizing a cherished memory the picture of pure surrender which is presented as the essence of Beth's womanhood occasionally sets one questioning. The extraordinary final scene of *Old Times* suggests that it set Harold Pinter questioning as well.

Structurally the biggest surprise about *Old Times* is that the plot is one that Pinter has used before, but with almost every element in it turned inside out or, as Claude Lévi-Strauss might put it, subject to a transformation. The earlier play is *The Basement*, performed on BBC Television in 1967; it remains one of Pinter's most resolutely minor works, but the parallels it offers to *Old Times* shed a curious light upon the dramatist's creative processes. In *The Basement*, two men find themselves in competition for a girl, who begins as the imagined property of one and ends as the property of the other; in *Old Times* a man and a woman are in competition, and the girl begins as the imagined property of both and ends decisively as the property of neither. In *The Basement* a man and a woman visit an old friend of the man's, at his home; in *Old Times* a man and a woman are visited by an old friend of the woman's, at their home. The two former friends in *The Basement* are the men, who become competitors over the third character; in *Old Times* the two former friends are the women, and the third character is one of the competitors. In *The Basement* the girl is young, and the context is for physical possession: the action covers a considerable length of time but hardly looks back to the past at all. In *Old Times* the two rivals compete for possession of the memories of a woman in her mid-forties: the action is compact, and does almost nothing but look back to the past. The action of *The Basement* is circular and ends (rather weakly) with the two rivals about to repeat the action, their positions reversed; *Old Times* leads up to a climactic scene which seems to ensure that the action can never be repeated.

In some instances, these parallels can be seen operating at a much more detailed level. Shortly after the opening of *The Basement*, when the girl comes in from the wet street, the first hint of rivalry between the two men appears in a polite argument as to which of the two proferred towels she should accept. Towards the end of *Old Times*, before the girl comes in from the bathroom the two competitors enter into a guilty alliance as they discuss joining forces to dry and powder her 'in her bath towel' (the words are repeated four times)[29]. In the earlier play the girl takes off her clothes and climbs into bed; she is offered a hot drink (which never materializes); in *Old Times* she enters wearing a white bath robe and sits on the bed, while the conversation harks back to sexual encounters of long ago; she too is offered a hot drink (which she accepts but does not drink).

Here the imagery has its connection with *Landscape* and one of Beth's reminiscences: 'I wore a white beach robe. Underneath I was naked'[30]. And *The Basement* has another link with *Landscape*. Fairly early in the television play, a scene takes place on the beach:

> *Interior. Cave. Day.*
> STOTT's *body lying on the sand, asleep.*
> LAW *and* JANE *appear at the mouth of the cave. They arrive*
> *at the body, look down.*
> LAW: What repose he has.
> STOTT's *body in the sand.*
> *Their shadows across him.* (p. 64)

Beth's second speech in *Landscape* begins: 'He felt my shadow. He looked up at me standing above him'[31]. This image, of a recumbent body watched by another, becomes central in *Old Times*. In *The Basement*, a man and a girl look down upon the body of one man; in *Old Times*, following the rules laid down for structural transformations by Lévi-Strauss almost to the letter, Anna recalls an occasion (which may, of course, be true or false) when one man looked down upon the bodies of two women:

> He stood in the centre of the room. He looked at us both, at our beds. Then he turned towards me. He approached my bed. He bent down over me. But I would have nothing to do with him, absolutely nothing. (p. 32)

It is a key speech, for the action described here is repeated, silently and exactly, in the final scene of the play.

It can be seen, then, that Pinter develops themes and images which recur from one play to another, in his most recent drama as much as ever before. The peculiar intensity of *Old Times* owes much to the way in which these personal images stalk through the play, investing scene after scene with added dimension.

But *Old Times* is more than a personal exploration of private themes. The arrival of Anna on her visit to Deeley and Kate and the triangular relationship that ensues give the play a firmly detectable though un-deniably enigmatic structure. There is a great deal that is mysterious about Anna. She can be seen in 'dim light' while Deeley questions his wife about her old friend in the first scene until, without a break in the action, she 'turns from the window, speaking, and moves down to them'[32]. A convenient stage device, to cut out the tedious business of in-troductions and small talk, or a suggestion that we are not to interpret her existence on a simple naturalistic plane? At the beginning, Deeley professes no knowledge of Anna, but in Act II he claims to remember her 'quite clearly' from 'the Wayfarers Tavern, just off the Brompton Road' and recalls the details of a party where he gazed up her skirt at her un-derwear[33]. Is Deeley simply engaged in a bid to devalue Anna's memories of the past, or is there some basis of experience in his account? Or is Anna's 'existence' taking fuller shape as the play progresses?

To ask such questions is rather like asking where Goldberg and McCann come from in *The Birthday Party*, and to wonder about the 'truth' of the various memories put forward by the characters is to go fundamentally against Pinter's intentions. Like *Landscape*, the play is not a fabrication of events, but of language and of essential psychological relationships.

Old Times is, among other things, a constantly amusing play, with Pinter's ear for the illogicalities of everyday dialogue toned down (as befits the upper middle class background of these characters) but ever-present. Anna's enthusiastic recollection of the past, when she and Kate were 'innocent girls, innocent secretaries', has a shade of parody about it, even when Pinter introduces one of his favourite themes:

> We weren't terrible elaborate in cooking, didn't have the time, but every so often dished up an incredibly enormous stew, guzzled the lot, and then more often than not sat up half the night reading Yeats[34]. (p. 22)

But the artificiality of her language is not a superficial device, for it mirrors the quality of her remembered experience, as the development of the play makes clear. Sometimes Anna uses words which are almost self-consciously archaic; on these occasions she is picked up sharply by Deeley. The first time it is casual and apparently trivial:

ANNA: No one who lived here would want to go far. I would not want to go far, I would be afraid of going far, lest when I returned the house would be gone.

DEELEY: Lest?

ANNA: What?

DEELEY: The word lest. Haven't heard it for a long time. (p. 19)

When the same thing recurs, we are prepared for it:

ANNA: Ah, those songs. We used to play them, all of them, all the time, late at night, lying on the floor, lovely old things. Sometimes I'd look at her face, but she was quite unaware of my gaze.

DEELEY: Gaze?

ANNA: What?

DEELEY: The word gaze. Don't hear it very often. (p. 26)

But this time the choice of word is more significant. In the next act, asserting that they have met in the past, Deeley turns the word 'gaze' back upon her:

DEELEY: ... I simply sat sipping my light ale and gazed ... gazed up your skirt. You didn't object, you found my gaze perfectly acceptable.

ANNA: I was aware of your gaze, was I? (p. 51)

Deeley's language, by contrast with Anna's, is blunt, assertive and inclined to coarseness, especially when he is roused. He is a subtle but characteristic specimen of Pinteresque manhood, violent in temperament but infinitely vulnerable in the end. Anna and Deeley are a well-matched pair, and their war of words as they circle cautiously around their claims to possession of Kate has the authentic Pinter flavour to it. In a sequence that has already become famous, they exchange nostalgic refrains from the romantic songs of yesteryear, once when their battle has hardly begun, and again as a sinister serenade when Kate makes her final entry[35].

In the fashion of Pinter's mature plays, *Old Times* is composed of themes which are taken up, dropped, reintroduced and woven together into a complicated pattern hinting at, rather than revealing, the mental workings of the trio. One notable sparring match takes place over a visit to the film *Odd Man Out*. Deeley gives a long account in Pinter's best narrative style of how, one hot summer afternoon, he first met his wife when the two were the only customers at a cinema showing the film:

> DEELEY: ... So it was Robert Newton who brought us together and it is only Robert Newton who can tear us apart.
> [*Pause*]
> ANNA: F. J. McCormich was good too. (p. 30)

Anna's response, an incongruous *non sequitur* involving an ungainly name, is one of Pinter's familiar comic gambits; but it is also a challenge, establishing that the memory of *Odd Man Out* is not in the sole possession of Deeley and Kate. And sure enough, a few minutes later, Anna is recalling an occasion when she and Kate:

> ... seized our handbags and went, on a bus, to some totally obscure, some totally unfamiliar district and, almost alone, saw a wonderful film called *Odd Man Out*. (p. 38)

Food imagery is well to the fore in *Old Times*[36]. There is a running joke about the possibility, mentioned by Deeley before her 'arrival', that Anna may be a vegetarian; this always appears in conjunction with a reference to the casserole that Kate has prepared for their dinner. Nor will it surprise readers that the contrast between the supposed vegetarian and the cooker of casseroles is always linked to a discussion of the marital ties between Kate and Deeley or Anna and her unnamed, absent husband[37]. In the most amusing of these sequences, while the drinks are being poured after dinner, the food theme becomes momentarily entangled with the naming process:

> ANNA: You have a wonderful casserole.
> DEELEY: What?
> ANNA: I mean wife. So sorry. A wonderful wife.
> DEELEY: Ah.
> ANNA: I was referring to the casserole. I was referring to your wife's cooking.
> DEELEY: You're not a vegetarian, then? (pp. 20–21)

When three characters are present on a stage and one remains largely silent, it is the silent one who is often most worth watching. This is certainly true in *Old Times*. As the curious competition between Anna and Deeley progresses, an attentive member of the audience gradually becomes aware that the elusive, self-controlled personality of Kate is a vital element in the play. Where the memories (true or false) of Deeley and Anna are precise and detailed, Kate is vague and non-committal. She has little to say about the past and appears to live in a dreamy world of blurred, indeterminate perceptions. 'That's one reason why I like living in the country', she says:

> Everything's softer. The water, the light, the shapes, the sounds. There aren't such edges here. And living close to the sea too. You can't say where it begins or ends. That appeals to me. I don't care for harsh lines. I deplore that kind of urgency. (p. 59)

There is only one concrete memory of Anna that she can summon up for her husband although that, as we shall see, may be less arbitrary than it appears. 'She used to steal things', says Kate:

> DEELEY: What things?
> KATE: Bits and pieces. Underwear.   (p. 10)

It is hardly surprising that Anna and Deeley should strive to impose a character invented by themselves upon an individual so unassertive: she becomes, almost literally, an 'object' of their affection. For Anna she was a girl sharing the pleasures of an innocent bohemianism; Deeley saw her as 'a slip of a girl':

> ... whose only claim to virtue was silence but who lacked any sense of fixedness, any sense of decisiveness, but was compliant only to the shifting winds, with which she went, but not *the* winds, and certainly not my winds, such as they are ...   (p. 35)

For much of the play Deeley and Anna exchange their memories of Kate almost as if she were absent. 'You talk of me as if I were dead', she says unexpectedly[38], and this expresses exactly the way in which the two compete, not of course for physical possession of Kate, but for her acquiescence in their own view of her.

Old Times tracks the way in which Kate asserts her own existence, but only at the painful cost of demonstrating a side of human nature which in its sexual aspects is decisively opposed to the lyrical reveries of Beth in *Landscape*.

The first major intimation that Kate is a more dominant character than we have been led to believe is linked to the references to Anna's theft of Kate's underwear, and Deeley's claimed memory of the time when he gazed up Anna's skirt. As the play moves towards its conclusion, Anna reveals that she had 'borrowed' Kate's underwear:

> Later that night I confessed. It was naughty of me. She stared at me, nonplussed, perhaps, is the word. But I told her that in fact I had been punished for my sin, for a man at the party had spent the whole evening looking up my skirt.   (p. 65)

This was the occasion of Kate's 'first blush':

> But from that night she insisted, from time to time, that I borrow her underwear—she had more of it than I, and a far greater range—and each time she proposed this she would blush, but propose it she did, nevertheless. And when there was anything to tell her, when I got back, anything of interest to tell her, I told her.   (p. 65)

Pinter's male characters derive peculiar pleasure from watching females cross and uncross their legs, and we are reminded of Ruth's lecture on appearance and reality in *The Homecoming*:

> Look at me. I ... move my leg. That's all it is. But I wear ... underwear ... which moves with me ... it ... captures your attention.   (pp. 52–53)

Here too we have evidently stumbled across another of Pinter's private themes[39]; but so far as the development of *Old Times* is concerned this strand of the plot has the effect of debasing both Deeley and Anna, whose life in London is seen to have its more sordid aspects. But above all it is the silent Kate with her aloof, enigmatic smile, who emerges as the most powerful of the three characters, and her final speech, when at last she is induced to reveal *her* memories, has an effect that shatters and humiliates both her listeners, reducing them unequivocally to the status of objects. 'I remember you dead', she tells Anna:

> I remember you lying dead. You didn't know I was watching you. I leaned over you. Your face was dirty. You lay dead, your face scrawled with dirt, all kinds of earnest inscriptions, but unblotted, so that they had run, all over your face, down to your throat.
>
> (pp. 71–72)

After 'quite a lengthy bath' Kate sat naked, watching her. Now the story turns to a man who, one may assume, is Deeley:

> When I brought him into the room your body of course had gone. What a relief it was to have a different body in my room, a male body behaving quite differently, . . .   (p. 72)

'One night', she recalls, 'I said let me do something, a little thing, a little trick. He lay there in your bed.' But instead of proving 'sexually forthcoming' she scooped some earth from the windowbox and 'plastered his face with dirt'[40].

Deeley *'starts to sob, very quietly'*; then, after approaching both women in the scene already referred to, he slumps in a chair; for a moment the stage lights come up sharply revealing the three still, silent and apart, a picture of death within life.

Lighting, it might be added, is used with great emphasis in *Old Times*, and this may be linked to the references in the text to 'gazing' and to the recurrent theme of one person standing over another, watching. Medusa-like, the characters of *Old Times* destroy each other with a glance, and the harsh light of the closing scene is (literally) a brilliant metaphor for this agency.

The climax of *Old Times* is one of those scenes that no amount of analysis can fully explain away. At its heart lies the contrast between purity and depravity, expressed in stage terms in the opposition between Kate's appearance as she enters fresh from her bath in a white robe, and her talk of mud and dirt; this is echoed in a minor key by Deeley's idealized picture of his wife[41] set against his furtive lechery in relation to Anna. As well as the succession of Pinter's female characters who are seen or described naked beneath a white robe after bathing, we are reminded of Flora's sexual encounter with the poacher in *A Slight Ache* ('up to my ears in mud'). It may be, as Martin Esslin suggests, that Kate 'has the superiority of the frigid wife for whom sensuality has no meaning'[42]; but it seems preferable to give the scene a wider frame of reference, and see it as Pinter's bringing together, by means of theatrical imagery, of the irreconcilable aspects of sexuality—attraction and revulsion, beauty and dirt, possession and destruction.

Old Times resembles one of those trick pictures which changes its nature according to your viewpoint. Seen from one angle, it is the slightest of comedies; seen from another, it is the darkest of contemporary tragedies. It has undoubtedly left some critics unsatisfied[43]; but it seems to me that here, more firmly than ever before, Pinter's portrayal of the irrational looks into the deepest recesses of the human psyche, and that the climax of *Old Times* is something of magnificent and unnerving beauty.

Notes to Chapter 4

1 *Daily Telegraph*, May 20, 1958
2 *Sunday Times*, May 25, 1958 (The review is quoted at greater length in Martin Esslin, *Pinter*, pp. 19–20)
3 *Sunday Times*, January 31, 1960
4 *The Theatre of the Absurd* (revised edition, Pelican Books, 1968), p. 275
5 *The Plays of Harold Pinter*, p. 182
6 Ronald Hayman, *Harold Pinter*, p. 36; Simon Trussler, *The Plays of Harold Pinter*, p. 88, etc
7 *Pinter*, p. 43
8 p. 43
9 p. 26
10 p. 49
11 p. 63
12 p. 74
13 *Pinter*, pp. 196 *ff.*
14 On this theme see particularly Walter Kerr, *Columbia Essays on Modern writers No. 27: Harold Pinter* (New York & London, 1967)
15 *Cf.* pp. 43. 59. 76, 78
16 p. 20
17 p. 32
18 p. 68
19 *Cf.* Martin Esslin, *Pinter*, pp. 46–47
20 "Harold Pinter Replies" (interview with Harry Thompson), *New Theatre Magazine* II.2 (1961), p. 9
21 *Pinter*, p. 169
22 p. 12–13
23 The term 'comedy of menace' was coined in 1957 by playwright David Campton to define his own work, but was soon applied more widely
24 p. 19
25 *Pinter*, pp. 88–89
26 pp. 18–21
27 Walter Kerr makes some illuminating comments on this aspect of the writer's stagecraft in his essay on Harold Pinter
28 pp. 12, 20, 24
29 p. 55
30 p. 13
31 p. 10
32 p. 17
33 pp. 48–51
34 *Cf. The Basement*, p. 68, where Stott, in one of the few references to the past, reminds his friend of 'those nights reading Proust'
35 pp. 27–29, 57–58
36 Much more so than in *The Basement*, although even in that play the turning-point is marked by Jane's cry of 'Lunch is up!' (p. 66)
37 pp. 12, 14, 20–21 and 40–41; *cf.* p. 67
38 p. 34
39 It is interesting to recall the reason which Davies in *The Caretaker* gives for leaving his wife: 'Fortnight after I married her, no, not so much as that, no more than a week, I took the lid off a saucepan, you know what was in it? A pile of her underclothing, unwashed. The pan for vegetables, it was.' (p. 9)
40 pp. 72–73
41 p. 31, etc
42 *Pinter*, p. 189
43 See for instance Kenneth Hurren (*The Spectator*, June 12, 1971)—'just another memory play'—or Simon Trussler (*The Plays of Harold Pinter*, p. 178)—'over-reliance upon the tricks of his trade'

Postscript

In the opening Chapter I declared that it was too early to pass definitive judgement on any of the three dramatists discussed in these pages; nevertheless, it would be carrying reticence beyond the bounds of duty to lay down my pen without offering a few tentative conclusions.

One thing at least, I hope, has emerged; Osborne, Arden and Pinter are far from being figures of the past. Although the popular imagination may associate them with the theatrical decade that was inaugurated by *Look Back in Anger* in 1956 (an impression that is coming to be reinforced by regular revivals of their early works), in fact they are still active playwrights exploring, innovating and, arguably, now writing much better plays than their earlier and more famous ones. It is true that a new generation of dramatists has entered the arena, successfully reflecting the diverse nature of the later 1960s and early 1970s (the varied talents of David Storey, Edward Bond, Tom Stoppard and Howard Brenton come to mind), while our three dramatists seem to have withdrawn to some extent from the sometimes turbulent, sometimes sluggish mainstream of the contemporary theatre; but it would be wrong to regard them as somehow replaced or superseded on that account. As I hope I have shown, their later work grows out of the concerns and interests of their earlier plays, but in no case is it simply a refashioning or reworking of earlier themes. Osborne, Arden and Pinter are still contemporary dramatists.

If this study has provided some pointers to their artistic identity it will have achieved its aim; it must be confessed that it is much more difficult, and possibly not very useful, to predict what posterity, measuring everything against a longer and more objective yardstick, will make of them.

Each of the three attracted critical attention to begin with because, in their different ways, they were innovators. John Osborne released naturalistic drama from its English tradition of well-mannered restraint; Arden created a new relationship between verse and prose in the drama, and together with Margaretta D'Arcy explored one theatrical form after another in his quest for an adequate vehicle for his wide-ranging view of society; while Pinter stripped dramatic form down to its bare essentials and, with what remained, exposed new areas of theatricality that possessed the rare quality of seeming distinctly personal and yet full of archetypal reverberations. But the attractions of innovation and originality do not last for ever, and there is no denying that all three of our dramatists are not without artistic blemishes of a kind which, as the years go by, could stand out with increasingly painful emphasis. It may be, therefore, that the stern judgement of time will dismiss these three English playwrights as marginal figures in the history of modern drama. I think this would be a considerable injustice, partly for the reasons I have given in my discussion of their work in the previous chapters, and partly because I believe that all three have made a significant contribution to the exploration of contemporary sensibility.

Osborne, Arden and Pinter are dramatists of so different a cast that it is difficult to explain how one person can possibly like all three. Osborne's strange vision of an England populated by a kind of reactionary counter-culture which devalues almost everything except the articulate nourishment of its own emotions reflects a scale of values diametrically opposed to the Ardens', who have moved progressively towards a view of the poet's role as a social one giving voice to the aspirations of the people, while the extraordinary mysteries that Pinter has uncovered within the recesses of the human soul seem to belong to a different world to that inhabited by an Osborne or an Arden character.

The freedom and diversity of the contemporary theatre to which I referred in the opening pages, and which the work of these three dramatists illustrates so amply, is not simply a matter of chance; it is a characteristic of our age, which combines a rejection of tradition and an adventurous determination to leave no intellectual, moral or emotional stone unturned with a basic sense of confusion and fragmentation of experience. The vigorous state of the English theatre in the 1960s has caused it to be compared from time to time with its Elizabethan counterpart, and critics have even wondered boldly whether, in the fullness of time, a latter-day Shakespeare might emerge upon its stage. But the nature of life in the twentieth century is such that no one artist can possibly sweep together so many aspects of thought and experience as did a Shakespeare; and this, it seems to me, is why we can respect Osborne without rejecting Arden, or admire Pinter without devaluing Osborne and Arden, and why all three dramatists will deserve the attention of future audiences. For each has succeeded in recording one aspect of life that jostles for attention in today's confusion. There is an authentic spark of contemporary pain in Osborne's rhetoric; there is justice in the Ardens' search for an alternative to Britain's Anglo-Roman heritage; Pinter's unique theatrical imagery has sounded the irrational heart of human relationships in a way that, for all his detachment from the contemporary intellectual scene, links him with some major strands of twentieth-century thought. The differences of our three dramatists, in short, do not cancel each other out so much as illuminate our troubled and fascinating times from different angles.

During the last year or so economic crisis has troubled the world, inevitably affecting that little corner of it with which this study has been concerned. The healthy state of the English theatre is now under serious threat: the ravages of inflation have left most of the subsidized theatre in a parlous condition, not simply checking plans for expansion but in many cases jeopardizing a theatre's very existence. The commercial theatre, too, has seen its audiences dwindle as domestic budgets become tighter and tourism enters a decline. Precisely how this will affect the careers of English dramatists already established it is difficult to see: new dramatists are certainly going to find it harder to get a hearing for their work in the months to come. Things look black; but one has only to glance through the pages of Richard Findlater's *The Unholy Trade* to see that economic difficulties are no stranger to the English theatre of the post-war years. The theatrical situation was almost as bad as it possibly could be in the early 1950s, and yet within less than ten years the English theatre had become perhaps the most vigorous in the world. As we enter the uncharted waters of the mid-1970s, it is impossible to know whether history will repeat itself: one can only cross one's fingers and hope that, whatever happens, the voices of Osborne, Arden, Pinter and their fellow dramatists will not be stifled.

Playlists

The dates given are the dates of first performance, except for unperformed plays, where the date is the date of first publication.

JOHN OSBORNE (born 1929)

Look Back in Anger, 1956
The Entertainer, 1957
Epitaph for George Dillon (by John Osborne and Anthony Creighton), 1958
The World of Paul Slickey (musical), 1959
A Subject of Scandal and Concern (play for television), 1960
Luther, 1961
Plays for England (double bill comprising *The Blood of the Bambergs* and *Under Plain Cover*), 1962
Inadmissible Evidence, 1964
A Patriot For Me, 1965
A Bond Honoured (adapted from *La Fianza Satisfecha*, by Lope de Vega), 1966
Time Present, 1968
The Hotel in Amsterdam, 1968
The Right Prospectus (play for television), 1970
Very Like a Whale (play for television), 1971
West of Suez, 1971
A Sense of Detachment, 1972
The Gift of Friendship (play for television), 1972
A Place Calling Itself Rome, 1973 (Publication Date)
Jill and Jack (play for television), 1974
The Picture of Dorian Gray (a 'Moral Entertainment' adapted from the novel by Oscar Wilde), 1975
The End of Me Old Cigar, 1975
Watch it Come Down, 1975 (Publication Date)

Screenplay: *Tom Jones*, 1964

Adaptation: *Hedda Gabler*, 1972

All the plays are published by Faber & Faber in separate editions, except for *Time Present* and *The Hotel in Amsterdam* (published together) and the double bill *Plays for England*. *Luther* is also published by Faber in an edition with an Introduction and Notes by Neville Denny (1971).

JOHN ARDEN (born 1930)

The Waters of Babylon, 1957; (*Three Plays*, Penguin Books, 1964)

Soldier, Soldier (play for television), 1957; (*Soldier, Soldier and other Plays*, Methuen, 1967)

When is a Door not a Door? (one act), 1958; (*Soldier, Soldier and other Plays*, Methuen, 1967)

Live Like Pigs, 1958; (*Three Plays*, Penguin Books, 1964)

Serjeant Musgrave's Dance, 1959; (Methuen, 1960)

The Happy Haven (with Margaretta D'Arcy), 1960; (*Three Plays*, Penguin Books, 1964)

The Business of Good Government (one act, with Margaretta D'Arcy), 1960; (Methuen, 1963)

Wet Fish (play for television), 1961; (*Soldier, Soldier and other Plays*, Penguin Books, 1964)

The Workhouse Donkey, 1963; (Methuen, 1966)

Ironhand (adaptation of *Goetz von Berlichingen*, by Goethe), 1963; (Methuen, 1965)

Ars Longa, Vita Brevis (one act, with Margaretta D'Arcy), 1964; (*Encore* XI.2, March–April, 1964 and *Eight Plays*, Book I, ed. Malcolm Stuart Fellows, Cassell, 1965)

Armstrong's Last Goodnight, 1964; (Methuen, 1965)

Left-handed Liberty, 1965; (Methuen, 1965)

Friday's Hiding (one act with Margaretta D'Arcy), 1966; (*Soldier, Soldier and other Plays*, Methuen, 1967)

The Royal Pardon (with Margaretta D'Arcy), 1966; (Methuen, 1967)

The True History of Squire Jonathan and his Unfortunate Treasure (one act), 1968; (*Two Autobiographical Plays*, Methuen, 1971)

The Hero Rises Up (with Margaretta D'Arcy), 1968; (Methuen, 1969)

Harold Muggins is a Martyr, 1968; (Unpublished)

The Bagman, or The Impromptu of Muswell Hill (play for radio), 1970; (*Two Autobiographical Plays*, Methuen, 1971)

The Ballygombeen Bequest (with Margaretta D'Arcy), 1972; (*Scripts* I. 9, September 1972)

The Island of the Mighty, comprising *Two Wild Young Noblemen*, 'O The Cruel Winter . . .' and *A Handful of Watercress* (with Margaretta D'Arcy), 1972; (Eyre Methuen, 1974)

HAROLD PINTER (born 1930)

The Room (one act), 1957; (Methuen, 1966)

The Birthday Party, 1958; (Methuen, 1965)

A Slight Ache (play for radio), 1960; TV version, 1960; staged 1961; (*A Slight Ache and Other Plays*, Methuen, 1961)

The Dumb Waiter (one act), 1960; (published with *The Room*, Methuen, 1966)

A Night Out (play for radio), 1960; TV version, 1960, staged 1961; (*A Slight Ache and Other Plays*, Methuen, 1961)

The Caretaker, 1960; (Methuen, 1967)

Night School (play for television), 1960, (*Tea Party and Other Plays*, Methuen, 1967)

The Dwarfs (play for radio), 1960; staged 1962; (*A Slight Ache and*

Other Plays, Methuen, 1961)

The Collection (play for television), 1961; (Methuen, 1964)

The Lover (play for television), 1962; staged 1962; (published with *The Collection*, Methuen, 1964)

Tea Party (play for television), 1965; (*Tea Party and Other Plays*, Methuen, 1967)

The Homecoming, 1965; (Methuen, 1964)

The Basement (play for Television), 1976; (*Tea Party and Other Plays*, Methuen, 1967)

Landscape (one act), broadcast on radio 1968; staged 1969; (Methuen, 1969)

Silence, (one act), 1969; (staged and published with *Landscape*)

Old Times, 1971; (Methuen, 1971)

Monologue (play for television), 1973;

No Man's Land, 1975; (Eyre Methuen, 1975)

Revue sketches and playlets (published in *A Slight Ache and Other Plays*, Methuen, 1961):

Trouble in The Works, 1959

The Black and White, 1959

Last to Go, 1959

Applicant, 1959

Request Stop, 1959

   Night, 1969; (published with *Landscape* and *Silence*, Methuen, 1969)

Screenplays (published in *Five Screenplays*, Methuen, 1971):

   The Servant (from the novel by Robin Maugham), 1962

   The Pumpkin Eater (from the novel by Penelope Mortimer), 1964

   The Quiller Memorandum (from *The Berlin Memorandum*, by Adam Hall), 1966

   Accident (from the novel by Nicholas Moseley), 1967

   The Go-Between (from the novel by L P Hartley), 1969

Select bibliography

I have excluded articles and reviews published in journals and magazines, and included a few books in the General Section which sketch in the background to the postwar British theatre or throw light on the changes which have overtaken it. Books marked with an asterisk contain more detailed bibliographies.

(Books are published in London except where otherwise shown.)

GENERAL

* Michael ANDERSON, Jacques GUICHARNAUD and others, *A Handbook of Contemporary Drama* (Pitman, 1972).
Michael BILLINGTON, *The Modern Actor* (Hamish Hamilton, 1973).
Peter BROOK, *The Empty Space* (MacGibbon & Kee, 1968).
John Russell BROWN, ed., *Modern British Dramatists: A Collection of Critical Essays* (Prentice-Hall, Englewood Cliffs, N.J., 1968).
John Russell BROWN, *Theatre Language: A Study of Arden, Osborne, Pinter and Wesker* (Allen Lane The Penguin Press, 1972).
John ELSOM, *Theatre Outside London* (MacMillan, 1971).
Martin ESSLIN, *The Theatre of the Absurd*, Revised and Enlarged Edition (Penguin Books, 1968).
Richard FINDLATER, *The Unholy Trade* (Victor Gollancz, 1952).
Richard FINDLATER, *Banned! A Review of Theatrical Censorship in Britain* (MacGibbon & Kee, 1967).
Ronald HAYMAN, *The Set-Up: An Anatomy of the English Theatre Today* (Eyre Methuen, 1973).
Laurence KITCHIN, *Drama in the Sixties* (Faber & Faber, 1966).
Charles MAROWITZ, Tom MILNE and Owen HALE, ed., *The Encore Reader: A Chronicle of the New Drama* (Methuen, 1965).
Charles MAROWITZ and Simon TRUSSLER, ed., *Theatre at Work* (Methuen, 1967).
John Russell TAYLOR, *Anger and After*, Second Edition (Methuen, 1969).
John Russell TAYLOR, *The Second Wave: British Drama in the Seventies* (Methuen, 1971).
Kenneth TYNAN, *Tynan on Theatre* (Penguin Books, 1964).
Raymond WILLIAMS, *Drama from from Ibsen to Brecht* (Chatto & Windus, 1968).
Katherine J. WORTH, *Revolutions in Modern English Drama* (Bell, 1972).

JOHN OSBORNE

Martin BANHAM, *Osborne* (Oliver & Boyd, Edinburgh, 1969).

Ronald HAYMAN, *John Osborne* (Heinemann, 1968).

John Russell TAYLOR, ed., *Look Back In Anger: A Selection of Critical Essays* (MacMillan, 1968).

* Simon TRUSSLER, *The Plays of John Osborne: An Assessment* (Victor Gollancz, 1969).

JOHN ARDEN

Ronald HAYMAN, *John Arden* (Heinemann, 1968).

Albert HUNT, *Arden: A Study of his Plays* (Eyre Methuen, 1974).

HAROLD PINTER

* William BAKER and Stephen Ely TABACHNICK, *Harold Pinter* (Oliver & Boyd, Edinburgh, 1973).

* Martin ESSLIN, *Pinter: A Study of his Plays* (Eyre Methuen, 1973) [a Revised Edition of *The Peopled Wound* (Methuen, 1970)].

Arthur GANZ, ed., *Pinter: A Collection of Critical Essays* (Prentice-Hall, Englewood Cliffs, N.J., 1972).

Ronald HAYMAN, *Harold Pinter* (Heinemann 1968).

Walter KERR, *Columbia Essays on Modern Writers No 27: Harold Pinter*, 1967.

John LAHR, ed., *A Casebook on Harold Pinter's 'The Homecoming'* (Grove Press, New York, 1971).

* Simon TRUSSLER, *The Plays of Harold Pinter: An Assessment* (Victor Gollancz, 1973).

Index

Aldwych Theatre, *see* Royal Shakespeare Company
Alvarez, A., 62
Arden, John, 1, *6–9*, 15, *50–87*, 116–118; *Armstrong's Last Goodnight*,
51, 52, 58, 59, 62, *66–69*, 72, 78, 81, 82; *Ars Longa, Vita Brevis*, 58,
59; *The Bagman*, 52, 56, 57, 58, 60, 61, 62, 69, 80; *The Ballygombeen
Bequest*, 1, 51, *80–86*; *The Business of Good Government*, 51, 57;
Harold Muggins is a Martyr, 51; *The Hero Rises Up*, 52, 53, 60;
Ironhand, 66; *The Island of the Mighty*, 52, 53, 58, 59, *69–80*, 82;
Left-Handed Liberty, 51, 52, 58; *Live Like Pigs*, 6, 56, 57; *The Royal
Pardon*, 51, 57, 59, 60; *Serjeant Musgrave's Dance*, 1, 50, 51, 57,
61–64, 66, 67, 68, 69, 72; *Soldier, Soldier*, 57; *The True History of
Squire Jonathan*, 51; *The Waters of Babylon*, 54, 55, 56, 57; *Wet
Fish*, *6–9*, 10, 14, 18, 54, 56, 66; *The Workhouse Donkey*, 8, 57, 60,
62, *64–66*, 69, 72
Aristotle, 4, 6
Artaud, Antonin, 2, 30
Arts Theatre Club, 88

Barker, Harley Granville-, 3
Beaford Arts Centre, 51
Beckett, Samuel, 103
Billington, Michael, 21, 22, 37
Bond, Edward, 116
Brecht, Bertolt, 2, 54, 55, 80
Brenton, Howard, 116
Brook, Peter, 60

Campton, David, 106 (ref. 23)
Chekhov, Anton, 4, 101
Chichester Festival Theatre, 72
Cocteau, Jean, 2
Congreve, William, 55
Creighton, Anthony, 26, 34 (*see also* Osborne, John; *Epitaph for George
Dillon*)

D'Arcy, Margaretta, 51, 52, 69, 116 (*see also* Arden, John)
Darlington, W. A., 88